THE BIG SHOW

A History of the Circus

FELIX SUTTON

Garden City, New York

DOUBLEDAY & COMPANY, INC.

1971

Library of Congress Catalog Card Number 73-103778
Copyright © 1971 by Felix Sutton
All Rights Reserved
Printed in the United States of America

For
MARJORIE MILDRED ELMEDA COE
—an old girl friend of mine.

THE BIG SHOW

A History of the Circus

INTRODUCTION

BILL DOLL

I THINK I was born with show business in my blood—and of course the most exciting of all show businesses is the circus.

When I first came to New York from the West Virginia hills I got a job as a reporter on the old *Herald Tribune,* but fortunately I was soon fired. The next day I set myself up in business as a press agent.

My first important client was the fabulous Mike Todd, who became the "boy wonder" of the New York stage in the latter half of the 1930s. His first big Broadway hit as a producer was *The Hot Mikado.* Mike was a press agent's dream. No stunt was too outlandish for him. He and I worked together for many wonderful years—from *The Hot Mikado* and *The Streets of Paris* until his tragic death in an airplane crash in 1958 when we were promoting his fantastic motion picture *Around the World in Eighty Days.* I am extremely proud of a blown-up picture of Mike which covers nearly one whole wall of my office and bears the inscription: "You made me what I am today. I hope you're satisfied."

In 1955, John Ringling North asked Mike if he could borrow me for the opening night benefit performance of the circus. One of the first gags I thought of was to have Marilyn Monroe, who was then at the zenith of her movie fame, lead the Grand Entry sitting on the head of an elephant that was painted pink. This gimmick almost stopped the show before it got started.

The next year I became Ringling's general press agent. I was with them for 10 years, and I have been beating circus drums ever since—for the Moscow Circus, the Strates Shows, and, among others, the circus in its newest form: *Holiday on Ice.*

In spite of its ups and downs over the years, in spite of its many changes, whether it is playing in a big-city arena or under canvas in a small town, the grand old circus still keeps rolling along.

Pat Valdo, the veteran clown, once said to me:

"As long as there are acrobats, clowns, horses, and elephants—and children of all ages to watch them—there will always be a circus."

CONTENTS

THE BIG SHOW
A History of the Circus

Display #1

THE GRAND ENTRY

Everybody loves the circus. In all the world there is nothing quite like it. It is a fabulous wonderland of fantasy and fun—a merry mélange of African jungle and Wild West; of high-stepping horses, trained lions and tigers, wire walkers, jugglers, tumblers, acrobats, and clowns.

When all three rings are going at once, the circus is a gay and infectious confusion of color and sound, sawdust and star dust, beauty and the beast. So many things are happening, all at the same time, that it is a hopeless task to try to watch every act as closely as you'd like to. Your eyes keep hop-skipping back and forth from one spectacular to another, until you finally surrender to the sheer magic of make-believe. One minute you are holding your breath as the daring young man on the flying trapeze twirls through the empty air; the next you are laughing your head off at the delightful awkwardness of the dancing elephants, who seem to be having as much fun as you are.

There are no adults at the circus. As soon as the band strikes up its first note, everyone is a kid again.

Barnum was right when he called it The Greatest Show on Earth.

We think of the circus as typically Made-in-America. Yet the many diverse elements that make up the modern circus are the world's oldest forms of entertainment. The circus was born, more than 4000 years ago, in the dimly lit past of ancient China, Egypt, Greece, and Rome.

Picture this scene in the long-dead city-state of Knossos on the Greek island of Crete. The year is about 2000 B.C.

It is a religious holiday, and a crowd of some 10,000 people are jammed into a large stone amphitheater. On the smooth white sand of the arena below are six or eight young athletes, girls as well as boys. They are naked except for scanty loincloths. Their hard, well-muscled bodies are deeply tanned by the fierce Aegean sun.

At a signal, a gate under the stands is opened and a huge wild bull ambles out into the ring. His heavy horns sweep outward and upward, and are almost sword-point sharp. For a moment or two he is dazzled by the brilliant sunlight. He stops and stands motionless, bewildered by his strange surroundings. Then the acrobats begin waving their arms and shouting to attract his attention and infuriate him into action.

Suddenly he lowers his great horned head and charges the nearest boy. The acrobat shifts his position until he is squarely in front of the onrushing animal, his feet firmly planted, his arms outstretched. A split second before the enraged beast hits him, the leaper seizes its horns and sails over its back in a tumbling somersault. He lands in the arms of a catcher who had moved into position behind the bull. Flipping to his feet, he whirls around in time to catch the next leaper.

One after another, the athletes perform a continuing routine of leaping and catching all around the arena.

Cretan bull-leaping is the first animal-acrobat act recorded in the picture history of antiquity. It would be a sensation in any circus ring today. But no modern performers have ever tried this ancient daredevil trick, and none are likely to. The slightest slip would mean certain death. In Knossos, death in the bull ring was considered to be a sacrifice to the gods, but modern kinkers (circus lingo for performers) work for fortune and fame in this world.

Throughout all the towns and cities of Greece wandering bands of entertainers performed in the market places, in the palaces of kings, or in the amphitheaters. For the most part they were jugglers, ropewalkers, tumblers, and animal trainers.

The arts of juggling and tightrope walking are said to have originated in China, just how long ago no one knows for sure. When juggling three or four balls in the air began to look too easy, the jugglers substituted lighted torches or china plates. When walking across a tightrope got to be too commonplace, the acrobats danced on the rope, did back-flips, or walked across it on their hands.

The ancient Greeks were perhaps the first wild-animal trainers. They taught bears, and even lions, to dance to the music of pipes and cymbals. Long before the time of Christ, they trained horses to prance, dance, bow, and kneel in the *haute école,* or high school, style so popular in today's circuses. Although music is played while horses do their tricks, they do not respond to the rhythm or the tune. Instead, they obey signals from the rider which are so subtle that they cannot be detected except by an expert —a light pressure of the knee, a slight shifting of weight, a gentle touch of spurs that are concealed on the inside of the boot heels.

Wall paintings in old Egyptian tombs tell the story of the circus acts that amused the Pharaohs. They show contortionists, jugglers, tumblers, and sword dancers. Some of them picture male acrobats swinging girls around and around over their heads. In others, Theban kinkers have leaped up on the shoulders of an "under-stander" to create a human pyramid almost exactly like the ones we see under the big top today.

The Egyptians, too, were extremely adept at taming and training wild beasts. The Pharaohs kept African lions and cheetahs as household pets, allowing them to roam freely around the rooms of the palace. Often a big cat was chained to a king's chariot, and went into battle with him. Early accounts tell of lions being walked through the streets on a leash, behaving as docilely as dogs.

Modern animal trainers are at a loss to know how the lions were made so tame; and some suggest that the ancient wall pictures and written stories were greatly exaggerated. It is virtually impossible to domesticate a lion thoroughly, and entirely impossible to tame a tiger—although on very rare occasions this has been done to a certain degree. Both lions and tigers are trained to do tricks only because they fear their masters.

When you see a big cat in a circus ring snarling, clawing, and baring its fangs at its trainer, you can be sure that this is not just an act put on to give the audience a thrill. If the beast had not learned to be afraid of the trainer's whip and gun, he would happily kill the man in an instant. The next time you see a wild-animal performance, notice that the trainer never turns his back on one of his cats until he has thoroughly cowed it by cracking his whip or firing his blank-cartridge pistol—and even then not when he is too close. True, some of the older cats have become fairly docile, and with them the trainer will sometimes take a chance. But there is hardly an animal trainer in the circus world whose arms and chest are not liberally crisscrossed with scars. In fact, all circus acts are much more dangerous than the kinkers make them appear to be.

A cheetah, on the other hand, is fairly easily tamed, particularly if you get him when he is a kitten. Although he is a big cat, he has a dog's paws rather than a cat's claws. And when he is tamed he can be as friendly and harmless as a big dog. He is the fastest animal on earth, and can hit short bursts of speed up to seventy miles an hour. The Egyptians used them for hunting antelope and other game, as do many sportsmen today.

The Egyptian Pharaohs established the first menageries, or zoos. Lions, leopards, tigers, giraffes, elephants, rhinoceroses, ostriches, bears, buffaloes, antelope, and even crocodiles were kept in enclosed parks where they could be viewed by strollers in the big cities along the Nile.

But it was in Imperial Rome that the ancient circus achieved its most spectacular effects—if mass murder of humans and mass slaughter of animals can be called spectacular.

The word circus itself comes from the Latin, meaning round. It described the oval track on which chariot races were run. The Circus Maximus, built between the Palatine and Aventine hills in Rome, was undoubtedly the largest stadium the world has ever seen. It was nearly 2000 feet long, and could seat between 150,000 and 200,000 spectators.

In the beginning, Roman circuses were relatively innocent, if highly dangerous, entertainments. Men wrestled and boxed, and chariots thundered around the long course. The boxers wore leather gloves, called *cesti,* which were loaded with iron or lead. A well-hit blow could break a man's neck or bash in his skull. The wrestlers, too, tried to win their matches with holds that were intended to break their opponents' arms, necks, or backs. A favorite trick of chariot drivers was to hook a rival's wheel and overturn his chariot while it was tearing around the track at a reckless speed.

The drivers wore metal helmets for protection and carried knives in their belts so they could cut loose the reins and free themselves in case of such a smashup.

Trick horsemanship was introduced into the Roman circus by stunt men who rode standing up on two horses, with one foot on each. Such equestrian exhibits are still popular in modern circuses, and the style is called "Roman riding."

Trained animals were popular crowd-pleasers in the early Roman circus. Trainers developed a trick of taking an antelope such as an African oryx—which has long, straight upright horns that grow close together—soaking the horns in a softening solution, and twisting them together to make one large horn that appeared to grow out of the center of the animal's skull. This kind of mutilation was the origin of the fabled, but nonexistent, unicorn.

The circus in Rome was a sure-fire vote-getting device for ambitious politicians. About half of all the Roman citizens in the city were jobless idlers who lived on political handouts. Since each citizen had a vote in the election of senators and other officials, no public officeholder could expect to win popular favor except by giving the populace plenty of "bread and circuses."

Roman circuses were advertised well in advance by signs painted on walls and the sides of buildings boasting in lavish hyperbole about the number of animals that would be killed or the gladiators that would fight—forerunners of our modern super-superlative circus posters.

It was during this time that the circus parade became a standard preface to the big show. Starting from the Capitol, the procession usually wound through the city's crooked streets, past the Forum, and on to the Circus Maximus. Tens of thousands of Romans, who could not find seats in the crowded arena, witnessed the grand spectacular as it passed.

Even P. T. Barnum, who made the spectacle of the circus parade an American institution, would have had to tip his hat in admiration of the way the Romans managed it. Companies of soldiers, arrayed in their most glittering armor, marched ahead of the politician who was furnishing the show. The patron himself, clad in a shining plumed helmet and flowing purple toga, rode a gold-and-silver chariot pulled by high-spirited horses.

After him came hundreds of animals in cages. These were followed by scores of chariots and display wagons, to some of which were hitched elephants, buffaloes, and even lions. Behind them marched the performers—acrobats, riders, huntsmen, and gladiators. All of Rome turned out to make the occasion a gala holiday.

As the Roman circuses grew more popular, they became bloodier and more brutal. The people could no longer be entertained by simple, even if hazardous, exhibitions of skill. Over the years, the Romans became hardened to cruelty and wanton killing.

At first, only animals were slaughtered for the crowd's pleasure. Lions were pitted against deer and buffalo. Bears were taught to fight each other. Archers and spearmen, both on foot and horseback, killed the animals in wholesale lots. Packs of wolves and wild dogs were turned loose on terrified antelope and giraffes. As the predators tore their victims' flesh to bloody shreds, the thousands of onlookers split the pleasant Italian air with their cheers.

Then, even the killing of animals became too tame for the growing Roman lust for blood. To satisfy the public's taste for cruelty and brutality, gladiators replaced the boxers and wrestlers.

These gladiators were selected from among the strongest and most athletic slaves, and trained to fight with swords, knives, tridents, and spears. Almost without exception, the contests ended with the death of the loser. The most skillful fighters, who consistently won and thus managed to stay alive year after year, became popular heroes. Often they were given their freedom, along with a palatial home and a lifetime pension. Many of them became instructors in the gladiator schools and taught newcomers the skills of the arena. Obviously there was always a shortage of gladiators, and the schools were crowded with new trainees. Many slaves became gladiators of their own free will, preferring the long-odds chance of eventual freedom to a short life of misery in the sulphur or salt mines.

When individual life-or-death battles between two men became the most popular circus feature, a new kind of arena was designed that could give onlookers a closer view. Among the several that were built, the Flavian Amphitheater—which we call the Coliseum—was the largest. The ruins of the Coliseum still stand in the heart of the old city today, and is modern Rome's prime tourist attraction. It seated only about 50,000 people, as against three or four times that many for the Circus Maximus, but everybody could see the close-up action in all its gory details.

The fights between single gladiators eventually became battles-royal, in which dozens of fighters took part, and which ordinarily ended when only one man was left alive. The more fighters that were killed, the better the citizens of Rome liked it.

The Romans were the world's first great engineers, as witness their system of roads, bridges, and aqueducts some of which still stand in many parts of Europe. And they outdid themselves when they built the Coliseum. For example, the arena could be flooded, and a real-life sea battle fought by the soldiers and sailors of two opposing ships.

The engineers also designed a collapsible ship. Loaded with wild animals, it would be floated on the surface of the water. Then, by means of an ingenious combination of springs and levers, the ship could be made to come apart and sink, leaving all the animals to flounder helplessly about in the water and drown.

History tells us that the mad Emperor Nero schemed to murder his mother, Agrippina, by having a luxury yacht built for her in this fashion. When the yacht, with the queen mother on board, sailed out of the harbor of Misenum on its way to Antium, it collapsed on schedule. Most of the crewmen were drowned, but Agrippina managed to swim ashore safely. His clever plan having failed, it was necessary for Nero to have her assassinated a few days later by professional murderers.

The flooding of the Coliseum offered many other opportunities for (by Roman standards) fun and laughs.

Troupes of dancers or acrobats would be hired to exhibit their skills in the arena. All ignorant of their forthcoming fate, and eager to entertain, they would begin their performance. Halfway through, the water would come flooding in and engulf them. This act always rolled the customers in the aisles. The circus managers must surely have imported their entertainers from places far away from Rome, for certainly almost every Roman citizen had seen this tragic trick pulled off many times.

Mass slaughtering of humans began when mass killing of animals became too tame for Roman tastes. The first victims were deserters from the Army and convicted criminals who had been sentenced to death. These unfortunates would be driven into the arena and there trampled by wild elephants or run down and killed by lions. This blood bath reached its terrible peak during the reign of the insane Nero.

When Rome was burned, in A.D. 64, Nero blamed the Christians for setting the blaze. No responsible Roman of the day believed that the Christians were guilty, for their newly formed religion was founded on the principles of non-violence and non-resistance. Most thought—and most historians have since agreed—that Nero himself hired arsonists to do the job in order to clean out the Roman slums and make way for the grand new city that he was planning to build. But when the Emperor announced that the Christians would be put to death in the Coliseum, the mobs went wild with joy. This promised to be the biggest and best show yet.

It was certainly the greatest single massacre of innocents in all of history.

For several days, and far into the nights, thousands of Christians were herded into the arena, there to be ripped apart by lions and wolves. Some were sewn into animal skins and attacked by fierce hunting dogs. After dark, the Coliseum was lighted by the flames of human beings who were being burned on crosses.

The dreadful killing of the Christians must have been just a little too much for even the horror-hardened Romans to take. Never again was the Roman circus so bestial. When, four years later, Nero provided the final display by slitting his own throat, the games in the Coliseum began to revert back to fights between trained gladiators. The mass murders stopped. Acrobats, fire-eaters, rope-walkers, and trick animals once again became features of the show.

Then, with the final fall of Rome in the fifth century, the circus vanished into the long black night of the Dark Ages.

Display #2

MOUNTEBANKS AND MOUNTED MEN

FOR a thousand years after Rome fell, all of Europe slept as though in a trance. The once-great Empire was broken up into dozens of small, half-savage kingdoms— Franks and Burgundians in France, Ostrogoths in Italy, Vandals and Huns in Germany, Angles and Saxons in the British Isles. The magnificent Roman roads were overgrown with weeds and woods. Communications almost ceased to exist. A man could live a lifetime and never stray more than ten miles from his native village. Progress in art, literature, and the sciences ground to a dead stop.

The circus, which Rome had developed on such a spectacular scale, disappeared overnight. The great stadiums and amphitheaters which the Romans had built throughout their far-flung colonies crumbled into ruins.

But the spirit of the circus refused to roll over and play dead. Even in the darkness of the Middle Ages, small troupes of traveling performers journeyed over the narrow roads and footpaths from town to town to put on shows in market places or in the courtyards of feudal noblemen. These medieval kinkers were known as mountebanks. The name came from the Italian phrase *monta in banco*, which meant, roughly, "get up on a bench." It derived from the fact that the manager of the show would climb onto a bench to make his spiel and call together a crowd. In time, the bench evolved into a primitive stage on which the performances were given. Later on curtains were added to the sides and front. This was the ancestor of the modern theater stage.

The mountebanks juggled balls and knives, walked on tightropes, jumped through hoops, swallowed fire, did sleight-of-hand tricks, and exhibited trained dogs and bears.

As part of almost every show a pitchman sold medicines and magical potions to the crowd. Since there were no doctors in those days of almost universal ignorance, the medicine men usually did a land-office business. The nostrums they concocted were foul mixtures of dried and mashed-up roots, bugs, toad skins, bats' wings, and other equally revolting ingredients that were supposed to be able to cure anything from a common cold to the Black Plague. The worse the stuff smelled and tasted, the more potent it was considered to be. It is a tribute to the strong constitutions of the country folk of the time that they managed to survive such harmful medication. But then the death rate in the Middle Ages was so high that only the halest and hardiest lived to adulthood in any case.

These quack healers were the forerunners of the snake-oil peddlers and their medicine shows that provided open-air entertainment in the back country of our early American frontier.

Over the centuries the traveling shows were expanded into village fairs, and the form of the modern circus began slowly to emerge. Often the medieval fairs were sponsored by the church and were held on the feast days of the saints.

It was during the Middle Ages that the art of rope-walking—the performers were called funambulists—reached a height of skill and daring that has rarely been surpassed. Old engravings show daredevils performing on ropes that were stretched between church towers, or slanted upward at a giddy angle from the street to the roof of the town's tallest building. Reaching the top, the acrobat would turn around and slide down the rope at a furious rate, often so rapidly that the soles of his shoes left a trail of smoke. This act is still a circus favorite, and is usually billed as the "slide for life." Trainers taught dogs and bears to dance on tightropes. And there are stories, impossible as they may sound, of men who rode horses up and down slanting ropes.

All in all, the outdoor performances of the Middle Ages and the Renaissance, especially the English fairs, were gay and boisterous occasions. They made up a crazy-quilt of circus, menagerie, carnival, bazaar, and side show. Clowns began to appear on the scene, and puppet shows—including the first Punch and Judy—were invented. Human freaks—dwarfs, fat boys, monstrosities with two heads on one body or two bodies with only one head—were certain to rake in a flood of farthings over the counters of the exhibition booths. The fakes were there too, a plenty, as well as the genuine freaks. Apes, which ordinary Englishmen had never seen nor heard of, were presented as "African Wild Men."

While the motley companies of mountebanks straggled across England and the Continent from about the twelfth century to the eighteenth, another form of entertainment began to grow in popularity. These shows were centered around horse training and trick riding. Like the country fairs, they were shown outdoors in public squares, fields, and roped-off arenas. Expert equestrians mastered such stunts as leaping onto the back of a galloping horse and landing with both feet in the saddle—or riding on their heads—or racing around a track with one foot in the saddle and the other on the horse's neck—or leaning out of the saddle at breakneck speeds to pick up small objects off the ground.

Then, as it was bound to happen, a natural-born showman stepped onto the stage, a man who combined the best of both the carnival and the horse show. And the direct ancestor of the modern circus was born.

The name of this little-known genius was Sergeant-Major Philip Astley, late of King George's Royal Light Dragoons.

Philip Astley was born in 1742 in the little English town of Newcastle-under-Lyme. Although his father was the village carpenter and cabinetmaker, young Philip's one love in life was horses. He learned to ride almost as soon as he could walk. At seventeen he enlisted in the Light Dragoons, and less than two years later he became nationally famous as the hero of the battle of Emsdorf, during the Seven Years' War. Upon his retirement from the Army at the war's end, he began to travel about England giving exhibitions of his riding skills.

After knocking around the countryside for a couple of years with his wife—who was also an expert rider—Astley bought a field in London on the south side of Westminster Bridge and set up a permanent riding arena. One of his many original ideas was that of the circus band, which he used to attract crowds. His first band consisted of two fife players and Mrs. Astley, who thumped out a loud tattoo on a bass drum. Astley himself and his trick riding were the only entertainment. There was no admission charge. After each show, his pretty young wife passed the hat.

Astley's show was an immediate success. Before long, he was able to cover his riding ring with a wooden enclosure and charge admission. His advertised price was: "Seats, one shilling. Standing places, sixpence."

He called his new establishment the British Riding School. Later, as business continued to boom and he became more aware of the pulling power of publicity, he renamed it Astley's Royal Amphitheater.

Philip Astley was a ham of the purest vintage. Before every performance he sat astride a white charger, dressed in his beplumed dragoon uniform, directing passers-by to his show by waving a long cavalry saber, and describing the program that was about to take place in a booming voice that could be heard—so it was said—clear across to the Houses of Parliament on the other side of the Thames. He discreetly started the rumor that the Crown had granted him royal favor because, as a young man, he had once saved the life of King William III. The fact that William III had died nearly a half-century before Astley was born didn't seem to bother anybody. Humbuggery, it would appear, was not the exclusive invention of P. T. Barnum.

As his horse show became more popular with the London public, Astley began to expand. He added more trick riders, including comic acts. Then he got the great inspiration that was to revitalize the circus and begin to shape it into its present form. He adopted the ideas of the traveling shows of the mountebanks and added them to his own equestrian displays. To provide light diversion between the spine-chilling riding acts, he began hiring acrobats, ropewalkers, trained animals, and clowns.

When his original amphitheater burned in 1794, he built a fine new theater that could seat 3000 people. It had a riding ring in the center, a stage at one end, and tiers of seats for spectators all around.

The performing ring that Astley designed has always been the symbol of the circus. And the size of the ring has not changed from his day to ours. The three rings of the great Ringling Brothers and Barnum & Bailey Circus in New York's Madison Square Garden—or those in any of the small tent shows that travel around rural America —are exactly the same diameter as was the one that Philip Astley first created.

By trial and error, Astley determined that a ring forty-two feet in diameter provided just the correct counterbalance of centrifugal and centripetal force to allow him to ride a galloping horse around in circles while standing on his head in the saddle or balancing on one foot. Trick riders, over the years, have agreed that Astley's measurements were ideal. And the circumference of the standard circus ring will very likely remain the same as long as the Big Show exists.

Philip Astley was not a man to let problems bother him for very long. When rival circuses started up in competition, he either bought them out or hired away their stars. When French and Italian riders became the vogue in London, Astley gave his own performers French and Italian names. This is a custom that has lasted until today. Many a circus acrobat or high-wire artist who is billed as Signore Guisseppe or Mademoiselle Fifi was born plain Joe Smith or Sally Jones on a farm in Iowa or Alabama.

The greatest challenge to Astley's imagination came when he took his circus to Paris. After the first performance, the chief of Paris police reminded him that his license entitled him to give "only exhibitions on horseback."

"Very well," said Astley, "we will perform only on the backs of horses."

Whereupon he built a large platform, supported it on the backs of sixteen heavy draft horses, and used it as a stage for his acrobat and clown acts.

As do all originators, Astley had many imitators. One of the most successful of these was a man named John Bill Ricketts, who brought the first full-scale circus to America. In 1793, Ricketts put up a large wooden amphitheater on Market Street in Philadelphia, which at that time was the nation's capital. President George Washington and his family occupied a free box at the opening performance.

Washington, who himself was perhaps the finest horseman in the United States, was delighted with John Bill. Ricketts rode standing on his head, and danced a sailor's hornpipe in the saddle. He leaped from one horse to another through a hoop, raced around the ring with a young boy balanced on his shoulders, rode on the shoulders of two riders, each one on a separate horse, and stood with one foot in the saddle and the other in his mouth.

The President, who was a rather dour Virginia gentleman and rarely expressed pleasure in public, was said to have laughed out loud at the antics of Ricketts' clowns.

The two became great friends, and John Bill often accompanied Washington on his morning rides through Philadelphia's bridle paths.

"I delight to see the general ride," Ricketts told a friend. "His seat is so firm, his management of a horse so easy and graceful that I, who am a professor of horsemanship, would go to him to learn to ride."

The Ricketts circus was a sellout hit in America. He took it to New York and Boston, and such out-of-the-way towns as Hartford, Providence, and Albany. Wherever he went, he always played to a full house. But Ricketts' flair for showmanship proved to be his downfall. He put together a spectacular called "Don Juan," in which that notorious sinner was consigned to the fires of hell for his many acts of misconduct. In this instance, John Bill outdid himself. The hell-fires got out of control and burned down the amphitheater, sending Ricketts into bankruptcy.

Broke and discouraged, he sold his horses and equipment and set sail for England. His ship was apparently lost in a storm and was never heard of again. A few other English-style circuses tried to follow Ricketts in America.

But they all folded. Now the stage was set for the kind of circus that was American-made, and not a foreign importation. And when it evolved there was one important difference—a difference that was to stamp *made in America* on the circus for all time to come. In Europe, the Big Show had been exhibited in permanent amphitheaters and was built around the horse. In America, circus people led gypsy lives, constantly on the move from town to town, and performed under canvas tents.

And the magic drawing card was not the horse—but the elephant.

Display #3

THE PONDEROUS PACHYDERMS

W HEN I was a small boy, there were three socially acceptable ways of getting into the circus.

If you happened to live on a farm, as I did, you could use one of the free tickets your family got for letting the circus advance-man plaster up a poster on the roadside barn. But this was too easy. It was almost the same as actually *buying* a ticket, which no self-respecting West Virginia boy in my day would do except as a desperate last resort.

Secondly, you could sneak in under the edge of the tent. But this involved an element of risk. If you got caught by one of the roustabouts, you were a marked man. Besides, you would lose considerable face with your associates.

But the grandest and most glorious way of all to gain access to the big top was to carry water for the elephants. Not only were you privileged to see the show for free, but you were personally a part of it. You were one of the behind-the-scenes actors in the Greatest Show on Earth.

You could reach out and touch a clown as he walked by—and touching a clown, as every circus fan knows, is the world's best guarantee of good luck. You could listen to the strange chatter of the acrobats as they strolled past in their bespangled costumes, speaking French, Italian, Hungarian, or whatever baffling language they used to communicate with each other.

But the great big thrill—the thing that made circus day

even more tremendous than Christmas or the Fourth of July—was the fact that you were working with the elephants, not just gaping at them. When you gave a "bull" her bucket of water (all elephants, regardless of sex, are "bulls" to circus people), you gingerly patted her trunk or fed her a peanut out of your hand. For a fleeting few hours you were something like her keeper, and you basked in her elephantine glory. Without elephants, there might just as well not have been any circus.

It was a female African elephant, named Old Bet, and a shrewd Yankee showman with the unlikely name of Hackaliah Bailey, that put the first truly American circus on the road.

In 1815, Bailey bought his pioneer pachyderm from a ship's captain in New York for a thousand dollars. Legend has it that the captain was Hackaliah's brother, who had purchased the beast in London for twenty dollars.

Hackaliah took Old Bet to his home in Somers, New York, where he established a permanent headquarters for her. Then, for the next thirteen years, he exhibited her in most of the small towns of New England and New York State. Accompanied by a supply wagon, Bailey and his one-animal menagerie traveled the country roads from village to village in the dark of night—so that farm folks along the way could not get a free peek at this curious creature from across the sea, the likes of which they had never seen before. During the daytimes, he showed her in a big barn or canvas-walled enclosure. The admission charge was usually: "Adults 25¢. Children, one dime."

On more than one occasion, Bailey employed a bright, ambitious young teen-ager from Bethel, Connecticut, one Phineas Taylor Barnum, as his barker and ticket taker.

Sometimes farmers, who were often short of cash money, paid their way in to see the pachydermous phenomenon with fresh vegetables or other homemade products. On one memorable occasion a rural Connecticut Yankee gained admission for himself and his family with a two-gallon jug of farm-distilled rum. That evening, after the show was over, Old Bet saw Bailey take a swig from the jug.

About midnight, Hack and his helpers were awakened by a tremendous, ear-splitting thunder of squealing and trumpeting. Old Bet had consumed the rest of the contents of the jug, and had gotten herself rip-roaring drunk. She smashed a wagon to smithereens and scared off all the horses. Thanks to the fact that her feet were chained down, she did not escape to terrorize the whole countryside.

By morning, with the aid of numerous tubfuls of cold water, Old Bet was sobered up. According to Bailey, she had learned her lesson. She never experimented with a jug of rum again.

Old Bet made a tremendous fortune for her owner. She became such a popular attraction that Bailey later added other exotic animals, such as bears and monkeys, to his traveling menagerie.

With part of his profits, Hack built a luxurious tavern in Somers, which, with proper deference to the founder of his fortune, he called the Elephant Hotel. On the lawn in front, he erected a tall, granite shaft with a gilded wooden statue of Old Bet standing on its top. The Elephant Hotel, now called the Somers Town House, is a local landmark. And from atop her stone column Old Bet still watches over it. Today the ancient hostelry serves as a community center and houses a permanent circus museum. Somers proudly proclaims itself to be the "birthplace of the circus."

After her many years of triumph Old Bet came to a premature and tragic end. In the early 1800s many religious fanatics regarded any kind of entertainment—and especially the exhibition of such a prehistoric monster as an elephant—

as being blasphemous and sinful. One morning, as Old Bet was happily ambling into a small New York town to give her daily show, an infuriated farmer rushed up with a heavy-gauge shotgun. Shouting loudly that she was the dreaded behemoth of the Old Testament, he fired both barrels through her ear hole and into her brain. The grief-stricken Hack Bailey had her buried with all the honors that the star attraction of America's first circus deserved.

After Hack Bailey had blazed the trail with Old Bet, touring circuses burgeoned in the Eastern United States. And the worth of every circus was judged by the number of its elephants. The ponderous pachyderms always got top billing on circus posters.

One year, P. T. Barnum's flamboyant posters advertised that his show had "20—count 'em—20" elephants on view. A rival circus owner bought newspaper ads in every town where the Barnum show played to point out that if the suckers really bothered to count 'em, they would find out that "Old Humbug Barnum" really had only fourteen. The suckers bought tickets just the same. Even fourteen elephants— "count 'em—14"—made the show well worth seeing.

There is something about an elephant that has always fascinated humans. This may be partly due to the fact that the Elephantidae Proboscidea is one of the few animals that has come down to the present day virtually untouched by the changes of evolution from its distant prehistoric ancestor, the mastodon. Or perhaps it is because the huge beast just can't help looking like a fat clown as it waddles along in clumsy dignity. One of the most popular features of the Big Show when it plays New York each year is the parade of the elephant herd from the railroad yards in Harlem, down through Central Park to Madison Square

Garden. The sidewalks are always crowded, for the march of the elephants is a good show all by itself.

In the show ring, the big brutes balance delicately with all four outsized feet on a tiny tub. They play on seesaws. They carry flags, lighted torches, and sometimes even pretty show girls in their trunks. They make pyramids by putting their forefeet up on each other's backs, and when they parade around the arena, or through a street, the one behind curls his trunk around the tail of the one in front.

The elephant's trunk is so sensitive that he can pick up a pin with its tip. He can gently wrap it around a human and lift him into the air. On the other hand, if he is angry, he can smash a man to a pulp with one swipe of it.

Having been a circus buff since about the age of ten, and having written two or three books on the subject, I am usually admitted on a press pass when the Greatest Show on Earth comes to town. This privilege, not accorded to ordinary mortals, allows me to wander around the back yard, the working area of the circus, which the average paying customer never sees. A press pass is the adult equivalent of carrying water for the elephants.

A few years ago I was in the back yard watching a bull-man shave the elephants. Now the hairs on an elephant are about as tough as barbed wire. They would blunt any knife or cutting edge, so they are trimmed with a blowtorch. But even though an elephant's hide is about two inches thick (hence the term "pachyderm," meaning thick-skinned), it is fairly sensitive. After the blowtorch singeing the bull-man rubs it down with a soothing oil. The elephant enjoys the whole treatment, just as a man with a two-day growth of itchy whiskers enjoys a pleasant shave.

On this particular day a big bull named Rosie was impatiently waiting her turn, tossing wisps of hay up over her ample back and swishing her trunk from side to side.

"Ever ride on a bull's head?" the bull-man asked me.

I replied that I never had but that I had always thought it would be fun.

"Then stand next to Rosie and stroke her trunk," he told me. "And relax. When she lifts you up, grab onto her harness and hold on.

"Okay, Rosie," he said to the elephant. "Up with him." Or words to that effect. I was a little too excited at the time to remember his exact command.

As easily and softly as an arm going around me, Rosie's trunk encircled my waist. Although I weigh about 165 pounds, she lifted me as lightly as a feather and deposited me squarely on the top of her broad, flat head. I clutched her head harness and hung on. The one thought that flashed through my head was that I wished the kids back in Clarksburg, West Virginia, could see me now.

Rosie, of course, is still with the circus, and I go to say hello to her every year. I think she remembers me and is glad to see me. But then they say that an elephant never forgets.

It is true that an elephant's memory is amazing. Zoologists will tell you that in the animal kingdom a bull's intelligence is second only to that of a chimpanzee. An elephant learns tricks quickly and easily and remembers them for years after she has ceased to use them in her act.

There are two kinds of elephants, African and Indian. The Africans are larger, but they are generally more unreliable and difficult to train. As a result, nearly all performing circus elephants are of the Indian species. In India, elephants have been used for hundreds of years as work animals, which doubtless accounts for their comparative gentleness. Just the same, no elephant is a creature to fool with. Nobody should approach one unless the bull-man is on hand and gives permission. Even so tame and seemingly harmless a bull as my old friend Rosie could lose her temper for a moment and attack me for no reason at all, and without any warning. Experienced bull-men have no idea why elephants behave so capriciously. They simply put it down to "elephant temperament."

Except for a few of the appealing little "baby elephants," almost all circus bulls are females. This is because, about once a year, males develop what is known as a "musth" season. Not even elephant experts know what causes it. Nevertheless, it can make a male bull go temporarily insane. Even in India, working male elephants are kept securely chained during the periods of musth. Before circus men became aware of this danger, a great many bull-handlers, to say nothing of innocent bystanders, were trampled and mauled to death. Today, about the only male bulls you ever see are safely behind heavy iron bars in zoos.

One of the most notorious rogue elephants was a huge African male, named Hannibal, who was brought to this country by the Van Amburgh Circus in 1844. Next to the immortal Jumbo, he is said to have been the biggest bull ever seen in the United States. He had the nasty habit of going berserk—both in and out of the musth season—for no apparent reason at all; and he killed at least seven or eight people before he had to be destroyed in the interest of public safety.

But Hannibal wasn't all bad. One afternoon a tiger escaped from its cage and attacked Hannibal's keeper, a man named Joe Martin. The old tusker quickly picked Martin up in his trunk and held him high in the air out of harm's way until the big cat was roped and recaptured. Of course no tiger—nor any other animal, for that matter, except a man with a high-powered gun—can harm an elephant. That is why the elephant, and not the lion, is truly the "king of beasts."

Another legendary killer was a big female named Queenie, who was part of the elephant herd with the Adam Forepaugh Shows in the 1870s. Over a period of about five years, she killed eight circus employees, a small boy who was standing on a sidewalk watching the parade in Buffalo, New York, innumerable horses, mules, and other work animals—and she totally wrecked the menagerie tent during a sudden storm in Uniontown, Pennsylvania. Then, as unexpectedly as her viciousness had flared up, it died down. And Queenie lived a long, peaceful, and harmless life from that time on until her natural death many years later.

The most famous elephant of all time was P. T. Barnum's fantastic Jumbo. He was the biggest bull ever seen, either in or out of captivity. And certainly he was the only animal that ever added an authentic adjective to Webster's dictionary.

Jumbo—the name means roughly "Hello, there!" in the Swahili language of East Africa—was captured by native hunters when he was a small calf and shipped to the London zoo. There, during the next seventeen years, he grew to an astonishing size. At maturity, he stood twelve feet tall at the shoulders, weighed seven tons, and could reach an object with his trunk that was twenty-six feet off the ground.

Yet for all his vast weight and bulk, Jumbo was amazingly gentle. He carried London's children, as many as a dozen or more at a time, around the zoo's grounds in a large wicker howdah strapped to his back. He consumed outrageous quantities of apples, peanuts, cookies, candy, and any other goodies that the English small fry eagerly fed him. All these between-meal snacks were in addition to his regular daily diet of some two hundred pounds of hay, several bushels of corn and oats, a dozen or more loaves of bread, innumerable tubs of water and beer, and at least one quart of good Scotch whisky.

Jumbo became as much of a London institution as the Tower, Big Ben, or the Changing of the Guard at Buckingham Palace. No journey to the city was complete unless the visitor went out to the zoo to see him.

P. T. Barnum had often seen Jumbo, and naturally wished that he could add him to his circus. But it never occurred to him that the big bull could be bought. Even so, Barnum put in a bid for him in the unlikely event that the zoo would someday want to sell.

Then one morning in 1882, for the first and only time in his life, Jumbo went on a slight musth craze. The zoo's directors, fearing that the gigantic tusker would never again be safe as a children's attraction, astounded Barnum by cabling an acceptance of his offer.

When the news broke in the London papers that an American circus man had purchased Jumbo, England almost blew up. School children contributed their pennies to a fund to buy Jumbo back. Queen Victoria got into the act by urging Parliament to pass a law to nullify the sale. A legal action was brought in the British Chancery Court that would make it illegal for the elephant to be taken out of the country. But the court decreed that Jumbo now legally belonged to Barnum and that nothing could be done about it. The American circus tycoon was vilified in sedate London newspapers as a Simon Legree who would enslave a beloved children's pet and exhibit it as a freak. All this fuss and furor only added to Barnum's publicity. He saw to it that American papers put up an equally stiff fight to have Jumbo brought to the United States. The Revolutionary War nearly started all over again.

It was Jumbo himself who added the final colorful touch to the elephant battle of the century. When he was led from the zoo and the iron gates clanged shut behind him, he laid his 14,000-pound body down on the pavement, refused to budge, and shed whimpering elephantine tears.

Barnum's British agent frantically cabled New York: "Jumbo has lain down in the street and won't get up. What shall I do?"

The world's greatest showman cabled back at once: "Let him lie there as long as he wants to. It's the best advertisement in the world."

At long last, the circus people managed to get Jumbo on board a ship for New York. The big bull joined the Barnum and Bailey show during its opening week at the Garden.

Jumbo cost Barnum a total of $30,000. During the three remaining years of his life he earned more than two million dollars for his owners. Even though the circus posters pictured Jumbo as being nearer thirty-six feet tall than twelve, the customers didn't seem to mind this mild deception. They expected Barnum to exaggerate. American kids, like their British counterparts, took Jumbo to their hearts. He always led the parade, carrying a large American flag in his trunk and waving it from side to side. Wherever the show played, children lined up with dimes clutched in their eager little hands for a chance to ride on his back.

A Jumbo fad swept the entire country. Manufacturers came out with Jumbo hats, Jumbo cigars, Jumbo neckties, Jumbo bars of candy—and restaurants from coast to coast featured Jumbo pies and Jumbo stews on their menus. Even today, nearly a century later, anything that is extra-large is referred to as "jumbo."

From 1882 until 1885, Jumbo continued to pack 'em in. Then, like Hack Bailey's Old Bet, he met a sudden and tragic death.

He always traveled in a special railroad car with his best friend in the elephant herd, a midget Asiatic named Tom

Thumb. One evening after the show, as the two were being led down a siding to their car in the little town of St. Thomas, Ontario, a freight engine came barreling down the wrong track. Jumbo managed to push Tom Thumb out of the way, but the locomotive struck him head-on fracturing his mighty skull and killing him instantly. The engine was hurled off the track by the impact.

Barnum had Jumbo's skin cured and mounted on a wooden framework. For several years thereafter, the stuffed Jumbo, rolling along on wheels, continued to lead the Barnum and Bailey parade. Today, Jumbo's mounted skin, somewhat moth-eaten and a good deal the worse for wear, is in the Natural History Museum at Tufts College in Medford, Massachusetts. His skeleton is on display at The American Museum of Natural History in New York.

Probably the second most famous elephant in circus history was also owned by Barnum. This was Toung Taloung, the "Sacred White Elephant" which P.T. bought from the King of Burma for an alleged price of $75,000. Barnum had honestly supposed that "Sacred White Elephants" from royal Asian courts were, in fact, pure white. Actually they are a sort of albino, colored a light gray with pinkish splotches on their skins, and with pink eyes. For religious celebrations, Burmese and Siamese priests decorate them with splashes of red and white paint.

Naturally, Toung Taloung was a mammoth letdown to the dozens of New York newspaper reporters who had accompanied Barnum and Bailey to the New York dockside to witness his triumphant entry into the United States. For a few minutes Barnum stood open-mouthed in dismay as he gazed for the first time on his much-publicized, non-white white elephant. But the old showman was never at a loss for words, for any great length of time.

"Boys," he said to the assembled writers, "Mr. Bailey and

I have imported this beast at a great expense as a public service—to educate the people and to dispel the widespread belief that so-called sacred white elephants are totally white. But I would also like to remind you that God made that white elephant. If my partner and I had made him, he would be as white as the driven snow."

Adam Forepaugh, who was Barnum's chief circus rival in those years, took an ordinary African elephant, covered him with a heavy coat of whitewash, and billed him as the Light of Asia. When the Light of Asia was introduced at a special press preview, one of the reporters sneaked in a sponge soaked with kerosene and rubbed the whitewash off a large section of the "white elephant's" leg. The "white elephant war" quickly died down. The Light of Asia, finally relieved of his cumbersome coating of whitewash, was returned to the Forepaugh menagerie and given back his original and more comfortable name of Old John.

When fire destroyed the winter quarters of the Barnum and Bailey Circus in Bridgeport, Connecticut, during the early spring of 1887, Toung Taloung was led to safety from the blazing elephant barn. But once outside, he panicked, rushed back into the burning building, and stood trumpeting in terror until the flaming roof and walls caved in upon him.

Symbolically, it was a baby elephant that sparked the historic partnership of Barnum and Bailey.

James A. Bailey was a go-getting young showman who had just taken his Cooper & Bailey Show on an unprecedented world tour, pitching his big top in such unusual places as Brazil, Peru, Argentina, Java, Australia, and New Zealand. Upon the show's return to the States after two years of globe-trotting, one of Bailey's elephants, called Hebe, gave birth to a baby son. Since the calf was the first elephant that had ever been born in the United States, Bailey promptly named it "Young America."

The perky and personable baby elephant, only about as big as a Great Dane and with a six-inch trunk, became an overnight nationwide celebrity and a box-office sensation.

Barnum promptly sent Bailey a congratulatory telegram, offering to buy the elephantine mother and baby for $100,-000. Just as promptly, Bailey had the telegram enlarged to billboard size with a screaming headline: WHAT BARNUM THINKS OF THE BABY ELEPHANT!

Being a good enough Yankee horse-trader to know when he was licked, Barnum offered Bailey a partnership. If you can't lick 'em, he figured, join 'em.

Cooper retired from the circus business with a neat fortune. Thus began a unique association that endured until Barnum's death—and that still survives in the biggest show of them all: Ringling Brothers and Barnum & Bailey.

Display #4

TENT SHOWS AND SHOWBOATS

As soon as it became apparent, in about 1820, that Hackaliah Bailey possessed a large four-footed gold mine in the
person of Old Bet, about a dozen men from the neighbor-
hood of Somers rushed to get in on what was obviously a
good thing. None of these people had ever had any experience in show business. But they were shrewd Yankee traders
who quickly recognized the sound of opportunity when they
heard it knocking on the door.

The first of these pioneer circus people were John J. June,
Lewis B. Titus, C. Sutton Angevine, and Jeremiah Crane,
all from the little town of North Salem, New York. They
hurriedly got together a small menagerie of mangy wild
animals, hired two or three acrobats, dressed up a few
farm hands in clown costumes, gave their show the high-
sounding title of the Zoological Institute, and set out in a
small wagon train over the back-country roads.

An advance pitchman usually rode into a town a day
or two ahead of the scraggly circus. He tacked up handbills
in taverns and general stores and gathered crowds of the
curious wherever and whenever he was able to give them a
spiel about the wonders that were on the way.

On the morning of the show, a clown-acrobat led the
caravan into the stand by a few hours. First, he would climb
up on a barrel and blow a horn or ring a bell to attract
attention. Then he would do a few tumbling tricks in the

street or on the village green. While he was performing
his come-on act to collect a crowd, the red-painted and mud-
splashed wagons, which had been traveling all night from
the last town where the show had played, would come
rolling in. The circus people—owners, wagon drivers, performers, and everybody concerned—would then set up a
circular canvas wall. After the circus band (which usually
consisted of a bugle, a fife, and a drum) had blared out a
raucous overture, the show would commence.

There were no seats, and the customers had to stand
throughout the performance after they had paid their way
into the canvas wall-tent. If it rained, the show was post-
poned until the next day.

During the first winter, the Zoological Institute kept its
animals in various barns scattered throughout the countryside of southern New York and New England. But in 1821,
the owners rented a large building on New York City's
Bowery. Not only was this a good, warm, safe place to house
the animals, but it also provided an enclosed amphitheater
where the menagerie could be exhibited for an admission
charge regardless of the weather.

Before the decade ended, more than a score of small
wagon shows were touring the northeastern states. Curiously,
they all originated in a small area around Putnam County,
New York, and Fairfield County, Connecticut, the locality
from which Hack Bailey had first started out with Old Bet.

Then, in the spring of 1830, a man came along who
changed the character of the circus as drastically as had
Philip Astley or Hackaliah. His name was Aaron Turner.
And he made circus history by taking his show out on the
road under the first "big top."

Turner's round-top tent was a marvel of its time. It was
supported by a large center pole, measured ninety feet from
one side to the other, and had rows of wooden seats for the

customers. Now the show could perform in all kinds of weather as well as at night, for the canvas top protected candles and oil lamps from being blown out by the wind. The circus at last was assuming its classic role as the typical American-made form of ambulatory entertainment.

Aaron Turner carried a menagerie that included two elephants, three or four lions and tigers, a couple of bears, and a small troupe of performing horses. In addition to acrobats and wire walkers, he also hired a young storekeeper named P. T. Barnum as ticket seller and treasurer. From time to time, when for some reason an act could not go on, young Mr. Barnum smeared his face with burnt cork and did double duty as a minstrel singer.

During the next thirty or forty years, there was an explosion of circuses and traveling menageries. Hardly a town of any size east of the Rockies was without its circus day at least once a summer. Little wagon shows sprouted up like wildflowers on a warm May morning. To the names of Titus, Angevine, June, Turner, and Crane were added those of Seth B. Howes, Isaac Van Amburgh, Hyatt Frost, Lew Lent, Gerald Quick, Jesse Smith, Rufus Welch, John Robinson, and enough others to fill up a whole page in this book. All of them—or almost all of them—managed to make money. Rural America was going circus crazy.

Certainly one of the most remarkable circus personalities of that day was a clown named Dan Rice. He was the only kinker in the annals of the circus who ever dared to dream that he might be elected President of the United States. The truth was that he had a pretty good reason to think so. He was the personal friend of at least twelve Presidents, from Andrew Jackson to Rutherford B. Hayes—as well as Jefferson Davis, President of the Confederacy. Zachary Taylor made him a White House aide with the honorary rank of colonel. When Abraham Lincoln became over-burdened with the problems of the Civil War, he frequently summoned Dan to the White House so that the two old friends could relax together for an evening swapping jokes and spinning tall stories. The clown staged recruiting rallies, sold government war bonds, and gave a large part of his fortune for the relief of widows and orphans of Union soldiers.

Dan Rice had a remarkable talent that has probably never been equaled for its versatility. No matter what he tried, he just naturally seemed to be able to do it better than anyone else. In his early teens, under the name of Yankee Dan, he was one of the best-known jockeys in America. Four or five years later, when he became too heavy to ride race horses, he became a professional gambler on Mississippi River steamboats. One evening he bluffed a player out of a large poker pot, only to discover later that the man was Louis Napoleon, the then-exiled emperor of France. But money slipped through his fingers as fast as he raked it in over the card tables.

Bored with life on the river, Dan caught circus fever. Billed as Young Hercules, he played for a season as a strong man and weight lifter. After each performance, he offered to take on any man in the house in a boxing or wrestling match for a prize. It is claimed that he never lost a fight.

He trained a pig called Lord Byron to do a fake mind-reading act, taught an elephant to walk on a tightrope, and was the only performer who ever managed to train a rhinoceros. He was a superb equestrian and trick rider, and a talented acrobat. But it was as a clown that he achieved his greatest fame and became the biggest single drawing card in circus history. At the height of his popularity he had dozens of circus owners bidding for his services at $1,000 a week. Certainly no circus performer before, and very few since, ever commanded so princely a salary.

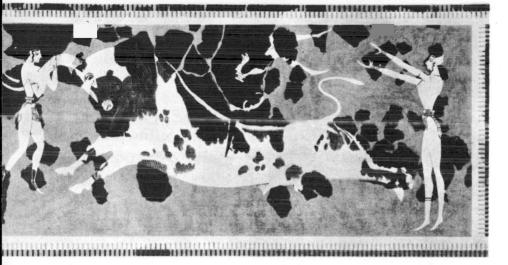

1. An ancient mosaic, unearthed from Grecian ruins, showing bull-leapers on the island of Crete. *(New York Public Library)*

2. Charley Baumann dances with Aparta, one of the ten Bengal tigers in his act. *(Ringling Brothers and Barnum & Bailey)*

3. The Circus Maximus in Rome. Nearly 2000 feet long and able to seat 150,000 to 200,000 spectators, it was probably the largest stadium ever built. *(New York Public Library)*

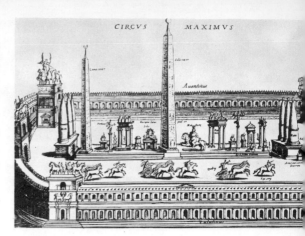

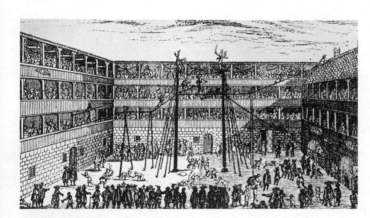

4. A medieval circus performing in the courtyard of a feudal nobleman. *(New York Public Libr*

5. Philip Astley's luxurious amphitheater in London. The size of the riding ring he designed is still the standard for circus rings today. *(Ringling Circus Museum)*

6. A "bull" practices her tricks in winter quarters.
All elephants, male and female, are called "bulls."
(*Ringling Brothers and Barnum & Bailey*)

7. An elephant's hair is as tough as wire.
Only a blowtorch will "shave" it. And the "bulls"
enjoy the treatment. *(New York Public Library)*

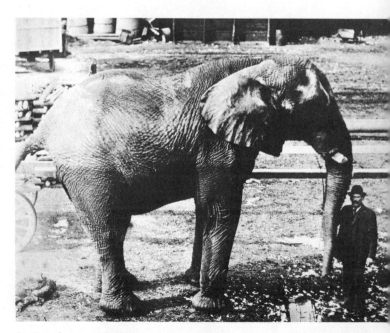

8. Jumbo was the biggest elephant ever seen, either in or out of
captivity. Although he was more than 12 feet tall and weighed
14,000 pounds, he was a children's pet. *(Robert D. Good Collectic*

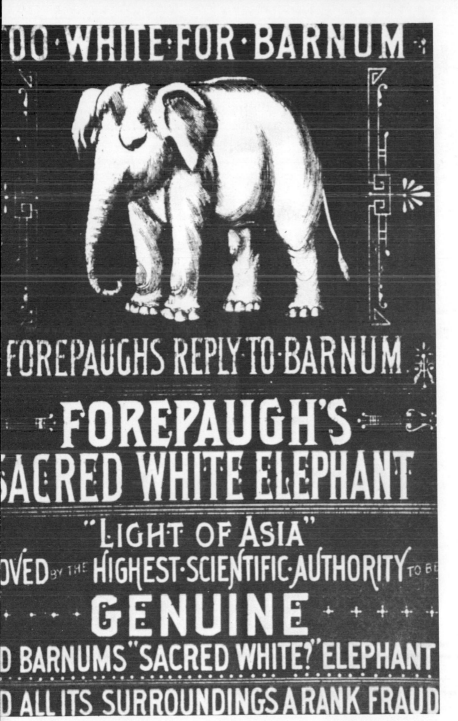

OO WHITE FOR BARNUM

FOREPAUGHS REPLY TO BARNUM

FOREPAUGH'S
SACRED WHITE ELEPHANT
"LIGHT OF ASIA"
OVED BY THE HIGHEST·SCIENTIFIC·AUTHORITY TO BE
GENUINE
D BARNUMS "SACRED WHITE?" ELEPHANT
D ALL ITS SURROUNDINGS A RANK FRAUD

9. When P. T. Barnum imported a sacred white elephant from Siam, a rival, Adam Forepaugh, painted an ordinary elephant with white-wash so that it would be even whiter. This is a typical "rat sheet" used by circus owners to call other owners "crooks."

(New York Public Library)

"WILL S. HAYS"

wo Steamboats used for transporting Dan Rice's Circus

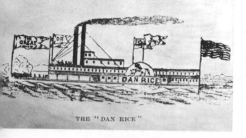

THE "DAN RICE"

10. Showboats took the circus up the Mississippi, Ohio, and Missouri rivers into back-country towns. During the war, some were allowed to move freely between Union and Confederate lines. *(Robert D. Good Collection)*

11. Captain Georg Constantine, as exhibited by Barnum in the 1870s. His entire body, even the soles of his feet, was completely tattooed. *(New York Public Library)*

12. General Tom Thumb, the famous midget who was P. T. Barnum's first million-dollar star. *(The Barnum Museum)*

13. The original Ringling Brothers. From the top: Alf T., Al,
John, Otto, Charles. *(Ringling Circus Museum)*

14. "Buffalo Bill" Cody at the height of his Wild West
Show fame. Chief Yellow Hand's war bonnet — his scalp
which Buffalo Bill "lifted" after their famous duel at
Warbonnet Creek. *(Museum of the City of New York)*

15. A typical small-town circus parade in the early 1920s.
(Ringling Circus Museum)

When Dan was still in his twenties, he was famous all over the country. He originated the Uncle Sam costume of star-spangled top hat and red-white-and-blue tail coat and trousers, and he grew an Uncle Sam goatee. He told political jokes that had a humorous twist. He wrote dozens of songs, mostly of a patriotic nature. He was the original personification of Yankee Doodle Dandy. Although he was a strong Union man, he had friends on both sides of the Mason-Dixon Line, and often took his circuses into the South even while the Civil War was raging. After each such excursion through the Rebel lines, he reported his observations and impressions to Abraham Lincoln.

In the era of the one-ring circus, when three different acts were not fighting for attention at the same time, Dan Rice ruled supreme as the King of Clowns. He always opened the show, and never failed to hold his audience spellbound. He told droll stories, declaimed long passages from Shakespeare, recited poetry, usually of his own authorship, sang songs, danced jigs, and exchanged ad lib wisecracks with the crowd. All America honored him—backcountry farmers along with such national figures as Horace Greeley, William Cullen Bryant, Stephen A. Douglas, and Robert E. Lee.

Dan took out half a dozen circuses of his own during the middle 1800s, as well as circus showboats which he floated up and down the Mississippi, the Missouri, and the Ohio to play the river towns. During some years he made a profit of well over $100,000. But he spent his fortunes riotously and lost them as rapidly as he made them. A supreme egoist, he insisted on bucking the powerful "circus syndicate" which was organized by a handful of New England capitalists in the mid-nineteenth century, and lost millions trying to fight it.

In 1868, after the radical Republicans in Congress had

failed by one senator's vote to kick President Andrew Johnson out of the White House, Dan began to think that his unprecedented popularity with all classes of Americans might well be enough to get him elected to the highest office in the land. To start the ball rolling, he founded a newspaper in his adopted home-town of Gerard, Pennsylvania, and ran for the state senate. However, he would not leave his show to campaign, and lost the election by a chin-whisker.

Nonetheless, a number of nationally prominent newspapers came out in favor of his candidacy for President, as did several prominent Washington political figures. "Dan Rice for President" clubs sprang up everywhere. But the idea of a circus clown as President of the United States was a little too much for the professional politicians to swallow. Besides, General U. S. Grant, riding high on the tidal wave of his glory as the conquering hero of the Civil War, was considered to be unbeatable. Gradually, the Dan Rice bandwagon slowed down to a rumble and a halt.

In the following years, Dan was at the peak of his circus popularity. He took a show on the road called the Paris Pavilion, the most elaborately staged circus ever attempted up to that time. He used a portable amphitheater with wooden walls and roof instead of a canvas tent, and he hired the most expensive talent that money could buy. But although he did a land-office business at every stand, the overhead was so tremendous that Dan lost a tidy fortune.

A year or so later he lost another one when the showboat on which he was taking his circus through the Missouri River country blew up, blowing up the whole show with it. Then came the final financial catastrophe. In the notorious Wall Steet "panic of '73," Dan lost every dime he had. From that day, his fortunes slid steadily downhill.

Always a fairly heavy two-fisted drinking man—even when he was performing as a boxer, acrobat, and trick rider

—Dan now began to hit the bottle with a vengeance. Adam Forepaugh, who was one of the most successful circus owners of the time, offered the famous clown a season's contract—and told him that he could name his own salary—if Dan would agree to go on the water wagon. Dan turned him down. Another circus man offered him a contract, again on his own terms, if he would allow his salary to be kept in trust until the season's end to guarantee his good behavior. All that Dan would have to do would be to come out and take a few bows. Again Dan refused.

For part of one year, Dan became a Temperance lecturer, speaking to groups about the evils of hard "likker." At the end of his talk, Dan customarily picked up a large water glass from the table in front of him, a glass filled to the brim with crystal liquid.

"Friends," he would say, "this is the natural drink God gave to mankind. Pure water."

Then he would drink it down.

The glass contained pure gin.

The great Dan Rice spent his last years in poverty, living on the charity of relatives and old friends.

During the forty years from about 1830 to 1870, the American circus business was dominated by a syndicate known as the Flatfoots. This organization grew out of the first group of circus men—Angevine, Titus, June, Forepaugh and others—which had sprung up in New England after the initial success of Hackaliah Bailey and his Old Bet. These men controlled most of the circuses then wandering through the Eastern half of the United States, as well as the showboats that plied the rivers. They bought up smaller rivals, took mortgages on little shows, and forced them into bankruptcy; they signed star performers to long-time contracts, and sent expeditions to Africa and Asia to collect animals for their menageries. They succeeded in bringing the first giraffe to America, in 1837, billing it as the Tremendous Camelopard. They built the first wagon-tank in which an African hippopotamus was trundled safely, sufficiently damp, from town to town.

This group of money manipulators was called the Flat-foots, it is said, because when a proposition was put to them that was not to their liking, they would reject it by declaring: "We put our foot down flat on that one."

Among them, they made millions. They could have re-tired after a few seasons on the roads and rivers and taken it easy. But the smell of sawdust and the lure of the circus trail were in their blood. They took their shows into the almost trackless hinterlands of the Midwestern frontier and down the rivers on showboats. They even ven-tured into the Southern states in the midst of the Civil War, and the people were so starved for entertainment that, although the showmen were Yankees, they were gener-ally accepted. Showboats were sometimes escorted past bat-teries of Confederate artillery by Union warships.

The most fabulous circus showboat of them all—and the forerunner of the later showboats that featured black-face minstrels and such melodramatic plays as *East Lynne* and *Ten Nights in a Barroom*—was the *Floating Palace*, the creation of a man named Doc Spalding.

Gilbert R. Spalding was a druggist in a small town near Albany, New York. A small circus that headquartered in Albany went broke and, as chief creditor, Spalding took it over for debt, whereupon he sold his drugstore and plunged into show business. He was a success from the start.

In 1851, he got the idea of putting his show on the water. At a cost of $42,000 he built the *Floating Palace*.

Nothing like it had ever been seen on the rivers before, and has not since. The *Palace* had a standard-size forty-two-foot riding ring, and was elaborately adorned with carved woodwork, luxurious drapes, thick carpets, and mirrored walls. It was lighted by gas jets, and could seat 2400 people.

The *Floating Palace* itself was a large barge which was pulled by two tow-boats. One of the tow-boats was the menagerie, which included an elephant, a giraffe, and assorted tigers and lions. When the water-borne caravan tied up at a wharf, the customers passed through the menagerie boat on their way to the big show on the barge. A few years later, Spalding added a second entertainment boat to his river fleet, the *Banjo*, which carried the first of the old-time minstrel shows.

The *Floating Palace* also boasted one of the first calliopes, an eardrum-busting musical instrument operated by steam and played something like an organ. It could be heard for miles. When Mississippi River people heard that screaming whistle, all work stopped and the joyous cry went up: "Showboat 'round the bend!"

In 1861, after the first battle of Bull Run, the *Floating Palace*, which happened to be in Southern waters at the time, was confiscated by the Confederate States Army for use as a hospital ship. Thus its glamorous career came to an unhappy end.

The circus is a make-believe world. Its present is fantasy and fairyland. Its past is folklore and legend.

But of all its legends, the most fantastic is that of a man named Phineas Taylor Barnum.

Display #5

THE ONE AND ONLY BARNUM

I<small>N THE</small> language of the ancient Hebrews, his first name meant "mouth of brass." And never was a man more aptly christened than Phineas Taylor Barnum. He has been called the greatest showman who ever lived, the Shakespeare of advertising, the master of ballyhoo. His was the magic touch of imaginative genius that changed the circus from a small wagon show, mud-slogging over rural roads, into the eye-popping spectacle that we marvel at today.

Barnum's name has almost come to be synonymous with the word circus. Yet except for one or two brief and ill-fated flings on the sawdust trail, he was never really a circus man until he was sixty years old and a semi-retired millionaire. Instead, he made his original reputation, fame, and fortune as a side-show pitchman on a grand scale— the promoter of the world's greatest collection of fabulous freaks, and a few fabulous fakes.

P. T. Barnum was born in the little town of Bethel, Connecticut, on July 5, 1810. He often said he wished he had been born a day earlier, because sharing the same birthday with the United States of America would have been an extra touch of personal publicity. And publicity was Barnum's lifeblood. He always operated on the principle of "I don't care what you say about me, as long as you mention my name." And before he died, at the age

of eighty-one, there was hardly a man, woman, or child
in America to whom his name was not a household word.

In later years, when Barnum's American Museum was
the most popular attraction in New York City, he was
delighted when the newspapers referred to him as the
Prince of Humbugs. And the public loved him for it. P.T.
was a master of psychology, the wizard of the practical
joke. He knew instinctively that people in that day of
scant entertainment liked to be fooled every now and then
—but not too often nor too crudely. When customers
flocked to the museum to see "the extraordinary cherry-
colored cat"—only to see a common black alley cat which
Barnum jokingly explained was the color of *black* cherries
—they could laugh at having been thus taken in, because
they always got more than their twenty-five cents' worth
from the hundreds of genuine curios that Barnum's agents
had gathered from all over the world. On only a few rare
occasions, did P.T. perpetrate a deliberate hoax. And of
these he said in his autobiography: "I was not proud."

Barnum's genius for making money with his brains instead of his brawn showed up at an early age. As a boy
in his teens he sold lottery tickets, a form of gambling
that was legal in Connecticut at that time. His "take" was
tremendous, but he began to spread himself out too thinly,
establishing lottery agencies in a number of surrounding
towns. When a few years later the Connecticut Legislature
suddenly and unexpectedly outlawed lotteries, he found himself buried under a landslide of debts and unpaid accounts. With the small amount of money that he could
scrape together, he took his wife and baby daughter to
New York and opened a little store in partnership with
a man named Moody.

Storekeeping bored him. It kept him constantly in a
state of mind that matched his partner's name. But at

least it provided food for the family table. Then one day, in the summer of '35, an old friend dropped into the store to say hello—and casually let fall a piece of news that was to set Barnum's feet at last on the road to his true destiny.

There was in Philadelphia, the friend said, an ancient Negro woman named Joice Heth who was 161 years old, and who claimed to have been George Washington's nurse. Barnum rushed to Philadelphia and was flabbergasted at what he saw. The old slave was toothless, totally blind, shriveled up, and almost completely paralyzed. Yet her mind was sharp, and she spoke clearly and intelligently. Her owner had a time-yellowed bill of sale which seemed to prove without a doubt that she had indeed been a slave in the Washington family at the time of George's birth.

Barnum bought her for $1,000, half of which he borrowed from Moody, took her to New York, and arranged to show her at Niblo's Garden, the city's most popular place of entertainment. He flooded the newspapers with ads, and customers stormed the box office. Auntie Joice, as P.T. called her, entertained with stories about "Little Georgie" Washington, and sang old-time Southern spirituals as she puffed on a corncob pipe.

When a newspaperman said to her, "Auntie, I have heard that smoking tobacco stunts your growth and shortens your life," old Joice replied, "Young man, I been smokin' for mor'n a hundred years, and it don't 'peer to have hurt me none."

Almost from the beginning, Barnum took in $1,500 a week or more with his antiquated curiosity. After a few months, when business began to fall off, he wrote an unsigned letter to the papers in which he suggested that Joice was not a human at all, but a cleverly made automaton; and that a ventriloquist was making her seem to speak. Again business boomed. People went back a second time to see how they had been fooled.

When the old slave died, an autopsy showed that she could not have been much older than about eighty. The press denounced Barnum as a swindler, but he contended to his dying day that it was he, instead, who had been swindled. The public didn't care. Fake or not, seeing old Joice had been fun.

Although he made thousands with Joice Heth, Barnum poured almost all of it back into advertising and promotion. Her death found him low in funds once more. But now the virus of show business was in his system, and he never got rid of it.

Within a month or two, he joined Aaron Turner's traveling circus. Then, when his contract with Turner expired, he took out a small tent show of his own. Because of the widespread prejudice against circuses as such in many parts of the Bible Belt, he called it Barnum's Great Scientific and Musical Theater. But the show went busted in New Orleans, leaving him with just enough money to get back to New York. Once again he was flat broke.

Then Barnum got the greatest break of his life—or, more correctly, he made the break for himself. By outwitting a group of confidence men who were trying to trick the owners of the original American Museum, he managed to buy the museum for himself—on credit and with no money down. Quickly he set out to transform its dust-covered collection of outdated relics into the most exciting show New Yorkers had ever seen. With his natural-born instinct for what people would pay good money to see, he began his lifelong practice of scouring the world for bizarre freaks. And when he found them he spared no printer's ink, nor any of his prolific penchant for propaganda, in promoting them.

Madam Josephine Clofullia, for example, was the original Bearded Lady. When Barnum signed her for his show she was married and had two children. The customers were interested, but not wildly excited, until a man named William Charr sued Barnum for fraud, charging that the madam was really a man dressed up like a woman. Barnum brought three of the city's leading doctors into court, as well as the madam's husband and children, to prove that Josephine was a female indeed. Thereafter, the Bearded Lady was a sensation and people lined up at the box office to see her—even after a nosy newspaperman revealed that Barnum had hired Charr to bring the suit in the first place.

P.T. had an especially soft place in his heart for giants. The public's favorite was Anna Swan, a pretty girl from Canada who stood seven feet, seven inches tall and weighed 430 pounds. She later married Captain Bates, another Barnum giant, and after the pair had saved up a modest nest-egg they retired to an especially built giant-size house in the country.

The Wild Men from Borneo were really two free Negroes from Brooklyn named Barney and Hiram Davis. They were nice, well-behaved young men, but when they were on stage they put on a fine show of snarling and growling and had to be restrained from attacking members of the audience.

Captain Georg Constantine, a Greek ex-soldier, was completely tattooed over every single inch of his body. He told Barnum that it had been done as punishment when he was a prisoner of bandits in China. Show-wise people generally agreed that the tattoo torture had been imposed at the captain's own request—probably by a tattoo artist in Paris or New York's Bowery—so that he could make an easy living without working. The customers came in droves, and gaped in awe. For all-male audiences, Captain Constantine displayed himself in the nude, to prove that when he said completely tattooed he meant *completely*. For mixed audiences, he modestly wore a loincloth.

P.T. introduced the first suggestion of the Wild West into show business when he induced a group of Sioux and Cheyenne Indian chiefs—who had come East to confer with President Lincoln—to appear at the museum. Their interpreter was well paid, but the chiefs had no idea that Barnum was charging admission to the huge crowds that came daily to see them. They thought the palefaces were streaming in to pay them homage. Barnum did not keep them long. He didn't want to push his luck too far.

In 1868, two men in Cardiff, New York, had a giant figure of a man carved out of limestone, artifically aged it with acids and dyes, and buried it in the ground for a year. Then they "accidentally" discovered it while digging a well. The scientists of the day were of two minds about the Cardiff Giant. Some argued that it was actually the fossilized body of a man from a long-ago age. Others loudly proclaimed it to be a colossal fake.

Meanwhile the two partners, William Newell and George Hull, were making money hand over fist by displaying their "Wonderful Discovery" to the curious who came from miles around. Barnum went to Cardiff, took one look at the stone monstrosity, and immediately recognized it as a gigantic hoax. But he also took a look at the line of people who were waiting to pay $1 each to see it. He offered the owners $60,000 for a three-month lease on the giant for the purpose of showing it in the museum.

When Newell and Hull refused, P.T. hired a sculptor to make a plaster duplicate and advertised it as the "Original Cardiff Giant." The owners of the first giant sued at once.

Barnum's defense in court was that since the original was a fake he was only showing a fake of a fake. He won the case, and customers kept coming to the museum to see Barnum's fake long after the Cardiff fake had been forgotten.

The master showman's most ludicrous put-on was what he grandly labeled the Fabulous Fejee Mermaid. This was a horrendous creature which had been manufactured in Japan—from the head and torso of a monkey which had been cleverly attached to the body of a fish—and sold to a gullible American sea captain. Barnum bought it for next to nothing after the captain finally came to realize how badly he had been taken in by the Nipponese taxidermists. He then proceeded to give it what was probably the most elaborate build-up ever foisted on the New York public.

The come-on began when P.T. planted stories in the newspapers to the effect that a remarkable mermaid had been captured in the Fejee Islands and was being escorted by a scientist named Dr. J. Griffin to the London Lyceum of Natural History. At the same time he publicly announced that he had attempted to borrow the mermaid for an interim showing at the museum, but that the English officials had refused to allow such a scientific rarity to be displayed for profit.

By the time Dr. Griffin—who was an old-time associate of Barnum's named Levi Lyman—showed up in New York with his precious cargo, public interest was at fever pitch. "Dr. Griffin" finally agreed to give a private showing for the press. The reporters, apparently, were thoroughly fooled, for their stories filled the front pages. At the height of the wave of curiosity about the exotic mermaid, Barnum announced that the London Lyceum had finally relented and would allow the scientific none-such to be shown at the museum for a limited time only "in the interest of public education."

Barnum had discovered long before that "education of the public" were magic words with which to draw crowds.

For over a year the grotesque Fejee Mermaid did a turn-away business. Nobody seemed to remember, or care, that it had been loaned by the British Lyceum for a limited stay.

P. T. Barnum's buzzing brain was never at a loss for new ideas. He organized the world's first baby show, the first beauty pageant, the first pet show, and any number of other promotions that kept his cash registers playing a golden tune. But his two most famous attractions over the years that he owned the American museum were Eng and Chang, the Siamese twins, and Tom Thumb, the mighty midget who made P.T.'s first millions for him.

Barnum bought the twins' contract from the captain of a Yankee clipper who had discovered them in Siam. They were an immediate sensation at the museum and, since Barnum paid them handsomely, within about ten years they were able to retire to a plantation in North Carolina. There they married the daughters of a poor white sharecropper named Yates, maintained separate homes (in each of which they spent half of every week), and between them fathered twenty-two normal children.

Despite the fact that they were joined together at the chest, Eng and Chang were as different as night and day. Chang was a heavy drinker, surly and ill tempered. Eng was a teetotaler who was always pleasant and well mannered. Oddly enough, Eng never felt any bad effects from Chang's continuous drinking. The twins spent thousands of dollars consulting the best doctors in both America and Europe, but since they shared several body organs in common, nothing could be done about separating them. Probably because they were doomed to be bound together for life, they hated each other with a deep passion. Sometimes they went for days without speaking.

One morning, when they were sixty-three, Eng woke up to find that Chang had died during the night. He too was dead within a few hours.

After the death of Eng and Chang, Barnum discovered another pair of twins who were joined together, back to back, even more closely than the Siamese boys had been. They were two Negro girls, named Millie and Christine, who had been born in slavery. P.T. headlined them as the Two-headed Girl. The sisters learned to dance, play banjoes, and sing duets. But apparently the novelty of joined twins had begun to wear off. The Two-headed Girl was never the shattering hit that the original Siamese twins had been.

Barnum took his single flight into pure culture when, in 1850, he brought Jenny Lind to America for a well-bally-hooed concert tour. Known as the Swedish Nightingale, Jenny was the most famous singer in Europe. When Barnum's agent first approached her, she hesitated to go to America under P.T.'s management because of his internationally known reputation as a purveyor of freaks. But the smooth-talking agent, plus Barnum's well-filled pocketbook and his generous guarantee, finally persuaded her.

The Nightingale played to packed houses everywhere she appeared in the United States. By auctioning tickets to the highest bidders and employing all the other promotional schemes that flowed so freely from his facile brain, Barnum made half a million dollars from the tour in less than a year. Miss Lind netted about two hundred thousand.

But Barnum made his first, and biggest financial killing with a remarkable midget named Charlie Stratton, whom he discovered quite by accident in Bridgeport, Connecticut, less than a year after he had opened his American Museum. The child had been born to normal parents, but had stopped growing physically at the age of about two months. When Barnum first saw him, Charlie was five years old and perfectly formed in every respect. Yet he was only twenty-three inches tall and weighed but fifteen pounds. He ran and played games with the other children in town, who seemed to pay no attention to his diminutive size. As if to make up for his physical proportions, the little fellow was unusually bright and intelligent and, as Barnum was to find out to his great delight, extremely talented as an actor.

Barnum hired him at once for three dollars a week, plus expenses for himself, his mother, and a tutor. In order to emphasize his smallness, P.T. advanced his age to eleven, and billed him as "General Tom Thumb, Just Arrived from England."

The tiny boy was an overnight hit. He danced, recited monologues that Barnum wrote for him, portrayed Dan Cupid, acted with the museum's giants in a David and Goliath sketch, and in general charmed the thousands who came pouring in to see him.

After two years at the museum, during which Charlie's salary was steadily and healthily increased, Barnum took him on a tour of England and the Continent. There he gave command performances for the Queen of England, the Emperor of France, and the royalty of virtually every other European country. Tom Thumb was an even bigger hit in Europe, if that was possible, than he had been in New York.

He traveled everywhere in an ornate carriage that was only eleven inches long by twenty inches high, and which was pulled by a matched team of miniature ponies that were of a comparable size. He starred in a play in London which had been especially written for him. He danced and sang "Yankee Doodle" for the delighted young Queen Victoria, cracked jokes with the crusty old Duke of Wellington, had his portrait painted by the foremost French artists, and received lavish presents wherever he went.

When he and Barnum returned to New York three years

later, P.T. took the boy into a full partnership—an association that lasted until Tom Thumb's death.

Between them they made millions. Charlie Stratton built a large estate in Connecticut for himself, and another one for his parents. He raised thoroughbred horses, sailed his palatial yacht on Long Island Sound, and married a lovely young girl midget, named Lavinia Warren, who was also in Barnum's show.

When P. T. Barnum was forced into bankruptcy several years later—through bad investments that were outside his natural world of show business and about which he knew nothing—Charlie volunteered to come out of retirement and go on another American and European tour. The proceeds put Barnum back on his financial feet.

In 1849, with Charlie Stratton's father as a partner, Barnum organized an animal show, called Barnum's Great Asiatic Caravan, Museum, and Menagerie. With twelve Indian elephants as its chief attraction, along with African lions, Burmese buffaloes, a loud brass band, a collection of curios from the museum, and an occasional appearance by Tom Thumb, the show went on the road. After four years of only moderate success, Barnum disbanded the circus and sold all his animals except one elephant. This one he took to his farm outside Bridgeport. There, with a man dressed as an Indian mahout perched on its head, the bull pulled a plow through Barnum's cornfield whenever a New Haven train went by. Passengers' eyes widened at the sight, and Barnum got pages of publicity on the possibility of elephants being the ideal work animals on American farms of the future.

Meanwhile, Barnum went back to devoting full time to the American Museum. One of his all-time favorite tricks was a pure gag, which nonetheless served a practical purpose. On weekends, New York workingmen were accustomed to bringing the whole family, complete with lunch baskets, and spending the entire day wandering around the museum. By mid-morning, there would be no room inside for those who were lined up at the box office waiting to get in. One night, Barnum had a sign put up over an exit door that read: THIS WAY TO THE EGRESS. When the over-stayed visitors rushed through the door to see what an "egress" might be, they found themselves outside the build-ing on the Broadway sidewalk.

On the zero-cold night of March 2, 1868, Barnum's museum burned to the ground, with the total loss of prac-tically all the animals, relics, and curios that it contained. The cause was a faulty furnace. It required three men to carry the Fat Lady to safety, and a few lions and tigers escaped and had to be hunted down and killed by the police. For a few hours, Broadway was crawling with snakes, some of them poisonous, that had gotten out of their cages. Fortunately, because of the extreme cold, no passers-by were bitten.

By this time Barnum had amassed a second fortune far greater than his first one. And when a man named George Wood offered to buy the Barnum name and goodwill for a new museum, as well as pay Barnum a thumping salary and a percentage of the gate to act as adviser, P.T. decided that it was time to retire to his Connecticut estate and live a quiet life of luxury.

The trouble was that Phineas Taylor Barnum didn't know what to do with his time when there was no colossal some-thing-or-other to ballyhoo. As Connecticut's most prominent citizen, he had been offered—but had refused—the nomina-tion for governor. He had served two terms in the legis-lature. With a partner, he had developed a new industrial and residential city called East Bridgeport which fattened his already swollen bank account. What would have been a full-time job for any other man, Barnum did with his left

hand. The aging showman could not hold still long enough
to enjoy the leisure that his years of hard work had earned
for him.

Sitting in his mansion in Bridgeport, champing at the
bit like an old fire horse waiting for the sound of the alarm
bell, Barnum got the idea of his life—the idea that was to
make his name immortal.

At that time, hundreds of small one-ring circuses were
traveling throughout the country. Why not, thought Barnum,
put together a show that would be the greatest, the most
stupendous, the most colossal, the most gigantic (Barnum
was never at a loss for exaggerative words) that the world
had ever seen? Accordingly, with a bright young man named
William Coup as his partner and manager, he organized
Barnum's Great Museum, Menagerie, Caravan, Hippodrome,
and Circus. It opened in Brooklyn on April 10, 1871, under
a tent that covered three acres, the biggest "big top" ever
seen up to that time.

During the summer, Barnum and Coup took the circus
on the road—"transported by 500 men and horses" as the
advertising posters said. That winter it played at the Empire
Rink in New York City. And while Coup took care of the
management, Barnum went back to Europe looking for more
attractions that would double the show's size.

The '72 circus, in fact, was so big that it was impossible
to transport it by wagon on the unpaved country roads. So
Coup hit upon the idea of traveling the show on rails.
Railroad-borne circuses had been tried before. But they had
never worked successfully for the simple reason that each
separate line had tracks of a different gauge. Thus, in a
journey of less than a hundred miles, it might be necessary to
unload and reload the entire show several times into freight
cars that fitted roadbeds of a different width.

By 1872, however, a standard rail gauge had been established which made it possible to switch cars from one line to another. Coup, who was the business manager, decided to play only the larger cities and towns and skip the small ones. Therefore audiences would be much larger and the box office a great deal more profitable.

The show took to the rails in something like seventy freight and passenger cars which were pulled by three locomotives. It was a sight such as no one had ever seen or imagined. Traveling by night, the circus could show each day in towns that were 200 or more miles apart.

Arriving at the crack of dawn, the show would pull itself together and put on a mammoth street parade at 8 A.M. While the performers and the menagerie were giving the citizenry a free and provocative look at themselves, the roustabout gangs would be setting up the tents—a huge one that seated some 2500 people for the main show, and a smaller one for the animals and side shows.

After the parade, the circus put on three daily performances at 11 A.M., 2 P.M., and 8 P.M.—a grueling routine that few other circuses have ever attempted.

In the fall, Barnum and Coup took the circus indoors once more, this time at the huge New York Hippotheatron. But on Christmas Eve Barnum's old enemy, fire, hit him again. The Hippotheatron was completely destroyed, along with the entire circus and all the animals except two elephants and one camel.

Barnum's loss was more than $300,000. But now nothing could stop the old master. As soon as he got the news of the fire, he began cabling his agents in Europe to replace all his livestock. And he gave them a go-ahead to spend an extra half-million so that the 1873 show would be even bigger and better than ever.

And it was.

The next year he built the Great Barnum Hippodrome in

New York, which occupied an entire square block and had seats for 10,000 people. A few years later, it became known as the original Madison Square Garden.

During the summer months, the enormous show took again to the rails and played under a canvas big top. By this time Barnum and Coup had dissolved their partnership, and Barnum went it alone.

He changed the name of the road show to Barnum's Great Roman Hippodrome and Traveling Circus—and for the first time employed the phrase that was later to become a legendary circus label: *The Greatest Show on Earth!*

Display #6

ENTER JAMES A. BAILEY

W HEN, in 1880, he used his baby elephant as a door-opener into a partnership with P. T. Barnum, James A. Bailey exhibited the shrewd hardheadedness that has prompted some circus historians to call him "the man who made Barnum." That nickname is something of an exaggeration, since Barnum scarcely needed anyone to manufacture him. But Bailey's sure hand on financial and managerial affairs left Barnum free to indulge his intuitive flair for pure showmanship. Between them, they staged the most sensational shows that had ever been seen. And never in any season did Bailey fail to wind up with a healthy profit.

Bailey's real name was James Anthony McGinnis. Both his parents had died when he was about six years old and he had struck out on his own, first as a hired farm boy and then as a livery-stable handyman. In the summer of 1860, at the age of twelve, he was working as a stable hand for a hotel in Pontiac, Michigan, when an advertising man for the Robinson & Lake Wagon Show came to town to "bill" the circus in advance of its scheduled performance. The press agent's name was Fred Bailey.

Bailey was so impressed with the energy and boundless enthusiasm with which the little stable boy worked that he employed him to help paste up posters and pass out handbills to Pontiac residents. Young Jim McGinnis, in turn, fell in love with the idea of the circus. When, a few days later,

Bailey left Pontiac to go to the next town on the route, Jim went with him. Before the year was out, Bailey had legally adopted the boy and changed his name to James A. Bailey.

From then on, the circus was James A. Bailey's life. Fred Bailey quickly faded from the sawdust scene, but his protégé went on to become the greatest manager of them all.

The youthful Jim Bailey's rise in the bespangled world of the circus was like the *whoosh!* of a sky rocket. At eighteen, he was bill-poster and assistant manager of Lake's Hippo-Olympiad. At twenty, after Bill Lake had been cut down by a drunken gun fighter in front of his ticket wagon, Jim hired out as general manager of the Hemmings, Cooper, and Whitby Shows. A few years later, Harry Whitby was killed just as Bill Lake had been—while arguing at the ticket window with a boozed-up gun slinger.

Always a careful man with a dollar, Bailey had saved his money. He bought out Hemmings' interest, and the show became Cooper and Bailey. He was just twenty-six. Subsequently, Cooper and Bailey absorbed the Great London Circus, Sanger's Royal British Menagerie, and the Great International Shows.

It was at about this point, while the circus was playing in San Francisco, that Bailey decided to take it on a chartered steamship to South America and Australia. Nothing so ambitious or daring had ever been tried with a traveling circus before. After surviving two or three South Pacific hurricanes—in which more than half of his big animals were killed or washed overboard—Bailey brought the circus back to the United States to a heroic welcome that threatened to overshadow Barnum. When Cooper and Bailey's Allied Shows opened in New York, two years after their adventures in the far Pacific, Bailey pulled another rabbit out of his hat. Much to Barnum's chagrin, the evening performances were illuminated by new-fangled electric lights instead of old-fashioned gas lamps.

At this time James A. Bailey was thirty-one years old. He was slightly built, beginning to bald a little on top, and he sported a handle-bar mustache and goatee. He weighed something like 130 pounds soaking wet. Outwardly he was shy and retiring. But inside, he was as tough as a kegful of tenpenny nails. This was the young man with whom Barnum came to grips over the ownership of the baby elephant —and whom Barnum decided to join rather than fight.

In the beginning, the new partners called their show the Barnum and London Circus. But they soon changed its name to the classic BARNUM AND BAILEY GREATEST SHOW ON EARTH.

The Greatest Show on Earth made its bow on Saturday, March 16, 1881, with a grand parade up lower Broadway that Barnum described, with his accustomed modesty, as "the most brilliant display ever seen in America." The entire circus marched up the street—elephants, acrobats, clowns, bands, the whole shootin' match—under the glare of calcium and electric spotlights. Broadway was jam-packed all along the line of march, and window space on the street was sold for as high as ten dollars per person.

Barnum and Bailey brought in newspaper editors and reporters from as far away as St. Louis and Chicago to witness the grand opening. It was, in Barnum's words, "a very costly piece of advertising, yet which yielded us a magnificent return." No circus had ever gotten so much favorable publicity.

After its New York stand, the Barnum and Bailey Circus hit the rails. The already immense tent area was tripled in size to accommodate the great crowds that poured into the show towns on excursion trains from places as far distant as fifty miles away. In most cities, the schools were closed in honor of "Barnum Day." Jim Bailey, the wizard organizer, always stood discreetly in his flamboyant partner's shadow. Barnum was the front man, the showman, the come-on. Bailey ran the business and counted the money as it flooded in an endless Niagara over the gate of the ticket wagon.

That summer and winter of 1881 inaugurated the first three-ring circus. "The only drawback," commented a newspaperman, "is that the spectator is compelled to receive more than his money's worth." While he watched a spectacular in one ring, the onlooker necessarily missed what was going on in the other two. As anyone who has ever been to the circus knows, three rings going on all at once are a little bit of too much. But Barnum and Bailey set the pattern. And Barnum had a reasonable explanation.

"Three rings guarantee a good show," he said. "If a spectator doesn't like what's going on in one ring, all he has to do is look the other way."

Except for European circuses which occasionally play America's larger cities, and which traditionally have only a single ring, any fewer than three rings looks like an old-time dog-and-pony show.

For the next ten years, the Greatest Show on Earth enjoyed an unprecedented success. With Bailey at the management controls, Barnum was free to roam the world for new talent and to enjoy himself. In 1889, the partners took their circus to England where, as the English might say, it was a "smasher." The Royal Family attended opening night. London's Olympic Arena, with a seating capacity of 15,000, was jam-packed for every performance.

Two years later, the one and only P. T. Barnum died quietly at his home in Bridgeport. His last words were: "Ask Bailey what the box office was at the Garden last night."

James A. Bailey carried on as sole proprietor. Even with

Barnum gone, the old master's pageantry continued to come through. The circus was still the Greatest Show on Earth.

Then one morning in April of 1906, while preparing for the season's opening in New York, Bailey took a stroll through the back yard to have a look at how things were going. There he was bitten by, of all things, a flea. Within a few days he was dead of an infection. He left an estate of eight million dollars.

Shortly thereafter, Bailey's heirs sold the show to the up-and-coming Ringling Brothers. But its name still lives today in the biggest and most splendiferous circus the world has ever seen—Ringling Brothers and Barnum & Bailey.

Display #7

THE BOYS FROM BARABOO

I T IS IN the best tradition of American folklore for a small-town boy to get circus-struck and develop a burning yen to join the kinkers under the big top. Thousands have actually done so. Hundreds still do. And a select few have made it all the way to the topmost rung of the success ladder. But never before nor since has a whole family of boys been so suddenly, simultaneously, and permanently bitten by the circus bug as were the brothers Ringling.

The father of this fabulous clan was a German harness maker named August Rüngeling, who migrated to the United States in 1848, married, anglicized his name to the more easily pronounced Ringling, moved from job to job in the Midwest, and finally settled down with his own harness shop in the little Mississippi River town of McGregor, Iowa.

By the spring of 1870, the Ringlings had seven strapping sons: Albert (Al), August (Gus), Otto, Alfred Theodore (called Alf T. to distinguish him from his older brother), Charles, John, and Henry.

It was also on a misty morning in the spring of 1870 that the famous Dan Rice brought one of his many circuses down the river on a showboat and tied up at the McGregor wharf. That was the day that shaped the Ringling destiny.

Long before dawn almost every boy in town, as well as a goodly cross-section of the men, had gathered at the landing. All of them were stretching their ears and straining their eyes for the first sounds and sights of the showboat. Among them were the Ringlings—all except Henry who had been born only the year before. Al, the oldest at eighteen, had promised his mother faithfully that he would take good care of little Johnny, aged four. Now he hung on to his brother to keep him from falling into the river or getting lost in the milling crowd.

Just as the first faint rays of the sun began changing the night into day, the music of the oncoming calliope swept sweetly over the water. And then, with huge clouds of black smoke billowing from her twin stacks, and all her lights blazing and her bells clanging, the boat steamed majestically around the bend and nosed gingerly into the landing.

A great yell went up from the welcoming committee. Then everybody backed off and watched wide-eyed as the crew of roustabouts began hustling off the circus equipment and hauling it to the show grounds on the edge of town. There were red circus wagons, golden chariots, long tent poles, mountains of canvas, cages of wild animals, scores of horses, a black bear with a ring in his nose. And last and most wonderful of all, the first elephant that anyone in McGregor had ever seen.

As the Ringlings walked home to breakfast, their eyes were full of stars. And when they arrived, an even bigger thrill was waiting. Their father was in his workshop repairing some broken circus harness. In payment, as was the custom of the times, he received free tickets for all the family. The performance that afternoon was all the Ringling boys needed to catch the circus fever once and forever.

Late that night, the Dan Rice show packed up and floated down river to its next stand. Everybody in McGregor forgot about it and got on with their everyday doings. Everybody, that is, except the Ringlings. No sooner was the steamer out of sight, than they began planning a show of their own.

Now in those days it was common enough for small boys to get up amateur shows for which the admission fee was usually one straight pin or two bent ones. But the Ringlings took their circus seriously. Gus, the second son was the only one who wasn't interested. He was too busy learning the harness-making trade. The other five, however, including four-year-old John, went at it hammer and tongs.

Al practiced juggling, balancing, and ropewalking. Johnny learned to sing songs and recite funny verses that Alf T. made up for him. Charles scraped away at his fiddle, while Alf T. tooted his cornet. All of them tried their hands at tumbling tricks.

By late summer they were ready. They rigged a makeshift tent from pieces of old canvas and put up a sign over it that read: RINGLING'S BIG CIRCUS. Then they opened for business. The admission price was one penny.

Amazingly enough, their first season of several performances in McGregor netted them the huge sum of $8.37.

All during the winter, the brothers prepared for their next year's show. Somehow they managed to acquire a sway-backed mustang pony and a scraggly old goat that they named Billy Rainbow. August made harnesses for them both. They salvaged a small wagon for Billy Rainbow and a larger one for the pony. These they painted screaming red. From settlers who were passing through McGregor in the wave of westward migration, they scavenged enough abandoned canvas wagon-covers to enlarge their big top.

After a year of tireless practice, Al had become fairly proficient at his juggling, balancing, and tightrope tricks. Charlie worked up a bareback riding act on the bedraggled mustang, from whose head harness waved a dyed-wool plume. Johnny, now a precocious five, had added to his repertoire of songs and jokes. If their tumbling acts were not perfect by professional standards, at least the aspiring young kinkers didn't fall all over each other so frequently.

Along about June they were ready to announce the opening of THE RING-LING CIRCUS. The show was preceded by a parade down McGregor's single street. Al led off with the red pony wagon. Otto followed with Billy Rainbow. The other three boys made up the band. When the procession reached the patched-up tent, Otto took over as doorman. The price in 1871 had gone up to a nickel. The Ringlings were on their way.

Unfortunately, however, the year 1872 was a bad one for August Ringling, Sr. He lost his business in McGregor, moved his family several times to towns in Wisconsin and Iowa, and at last to Baraboo, Wisconsin, where he set up his own shop again. This time for good.

Meanwhile the grandiose plans for a great Ringling Brothers Circus had been laid temporarily on the shelf. But even though the boys scattered, the circus dream kept dancing like a great big sugarplum in the backs of their heads.

Al went away to join a succession of vagabond shows that played one-night stands in town halls and saloons throughout the Midwest—as juggler, ropewalker, and sometimes manager. Alf T. and Charlie went to work for their father. Otto, who had also learned the harness-making trade, drifted from one job to another. John, always a chaser after rainbows, ran away from home when he was twelve and worked as a handyman, roustabout, and ticket taker for a number of shows that hopped, skipped, and jumped across the prairie country.

By 1882, twelve years after their first penny show, the Ringling boys figured they were ready. The clan gathered at Baraboo. Al, now thirty, was the leader. He had been working on his juggling, balancing, and ropewalking until he was an accomplished acrobat.

In the Ringling barn in Baraboo, they put together their show. Grandly and alliteratively, they billed it:

RINGLING BROTHERS
CLASSIC AND COMIC CONCERT COMPANY
Fourth Season—1882

How they arrived at the "Fourth Season" is not quite clear. They probably counted their amateur penny show of 1870 as their first; their nickel show the next year as their second; and perhaps Al's wanderings with various shows as their third.

They opened in a run-down hall in Mazomanie, Wisconsin, on a snowy evening in November. Their printed programs promised:

NEW ACTS!   NEW SONGS!   NEW DANCES!
NEW SAYINGS!   NEW FACES!

But all of the faces were those of the brothers Ringling.

The premier performance took in thirteen dollars. At their next stand, Green Spring, they got an unexpected break. A barn dance scheduled for that same evening had been called off for some reason or another. And all the farmers who had driven into town for the dance went to the show instead. The take was sixty dollars.

All the rest of the winter they straggled with their make-shift show through Michigan, Minnesota, and South Dakota. And in April they arrived back in Baraboo—dead broke.

But being broke never bothered the Ringlings. Somehow they managed to enlarge the show, and in August they took to the road again with:

RINGLING BROTHERS
GRAND CARNIVAL OF FUN!
FUN! FUN! FUN!

They ended the season with a profit of one thousand dollars.

It was the next year that the Ringlings began to roll down the glory road.

In his wandering with other shows, Al had met a veteran wagon-show man called Yankee Robinson, who, ten years before, had owned one of the most successful traveling circuses on the road. Reckless overexpansion, however, had ruined him financially and his circus had been sold to pay its debts. But his name was still a magic drawing card in the Midwest and the old showman was eager to get back under the big top. In 1884, he offered to throw in with the up-and-coming Ringlings.

During the winter months the brothers, with old Yankee Robinson to advise them, built a bigger show. They ordered a tent that could seat six hundred people; then they went into the pine woods near Baraboo and cut the tent poles themselves. Al's wife, Louise, whom he had married the year before, made the costumes. In later years she became a bareback rider and snake charmer. With the last of their dwindling capital, they hired a half dozen performers who could also double as members of the band.

On May 19, 1884, they opened their new circus in Baraboo under the title:

YANKEE ROBINSON and RINGLING BROTHERS
GREAT DOUBLE SHOW!

It must be admitted that the Great Double Show was not much better than the Carnival of Fun had been. But as Yankee Robinson led the small parade down the town's main street, he halted it at a corner where a crowd had gathered, took off his high hat, bowed, and proclaimed:

"La-dees and gennel-men! I am an old man. I have traveled every state of the Union—and soon I will pass into that arena of life that knows no ending. And when I do, I want to die in harness with my name associated with that of the Ringling brothers. For I tell you that the Ringlings are the future showmen of America."

The crowd cheered—and followed the scraggly parade to the show grounds where they filled the tent to overflowing.

The circus had no animals, not even a horse act. The boys juggled, tumbled, and did acrobatics. Al performed his ropewalking act. John was the one and only clown. When a section of the jerry-built seats collapsed, old Yankee saved the day by telling jokes, helping people to their feet, and restoring good humor all around.

As soon as the performance was over, the brothers shucked off their costumes, put on overalls, hauled down the tent, and pulled out for their next stand at Sauk City. Their equipment was carried in wagons rented from local farmers.

For the rest of the summer the Great Double Show struggled over dusty—or sometimes soggy and muddy—roads the length and breadth of the western Great Lakes country. By cutting corners and hoarding every dollar they could, the brothers managed to wind up the season with a small profit.

In August, the aging Yankee Robinson got the wish that he had expressed on the Baraboo street corner. He collapsed and died, still "in harness." But his experience and know-how had made the young Ringlings into reasonably seasoned circus men. Slowly, their show began to grow. It required fifteen wagons to haul the 1885 show, which by this time had a menagerie that consisted of a trained pig and a somewhat shabby hyena. The hyena got top billing, at follows:

HIDEOUS HYENA—STRIATA GIGANTIUM!
The Mammoth, Midnight, Marauding, Man-eating Monstrosity, the Prowling, Grave-robbing Demon of all Created Things, who, while the World Sleeps, sneaks stealthily under cover of Darkness to the Cemetery and with Ghoulish Glee robs the Tomb. His

Hideous Laughter paralyzes with Terror the Bravest Hearts. He leaves behind him a Trail of Blood, and the Wails of the Dying are Music to his Ear!

The rather moth-eaten Striata Gigantium (the name was Al's invention) may have been a disappointment to those customers who came to the show expecting to be paralyzed with terror. But the Ringlings were learning some of the tricks of crowd-pulling that had made a fortune for P. T. Barnum.

Year after year, the Ringling Brothers Circus prospered. Gradually they built up their menagerie to include elephants, camels, hippos, lions, tigers, bears, and other authentic wild animals. They hired acrobats, trick riders, and clowns. In 1890, they went on the rails with eighteen cars. Two years later they had thirty-one. By this time, Gus and Henry had joined the show, thus getting all seven brothers into the family partnership. The original five had long since given up performing and had divided up the various phases of management.

Al became the show's producer and director. Otto handled the finances. Charlie took care of advertising. Alf T. was the promotional genius and idea man. John became general manager. Gus was the advance man, and Henry functioned as superintendent, while often doubling as doorman and ticket seller.

In the heyday of the rural wagon shows, crooks and confidence men latched onto circuses like leeches, often with the consent and cooperation of the management. Some even paid the circus owners for the privilege of fleecing the country people who came to town for the big show. It was a common practice in some circuses for the ticket sellers to receive no salary. Instead, they made their money by short-changing the customers. Crooked gamblers and shell-game operators were a part of almost every old-time road show.

Pickpockets always had a field day. Some even went so far as to put up signs that said: "Beware of pickpockets!" When a local yokel saw such a sign, he instinctively patted the pocket in which he carried his wallet—thus pointing the alert "dips" to the exact location of his poke.

From the very beginning of their circus, the Ringlings determined to run a show that was completely honest. When various grafters approached them with offers to buy the privilege of stealing from patrons, the burly brothers threw them bodily off the lot. Before long, they got a reputation as a "Sunday school" circus—that is, an entirely clean one. They always gave every customer his fill of top-notch entertainment and at the same time protected him from crooks. In later years they employed the famous William J. Burns private detective agency to police their shows. The public was grateful, and showed its appreciation at the box office.

By the turn of the century, circus rivalry in America was at its height. The Barnum and Bailey Greatest Show on Earth was, of course, the biggest. But the Ringling Brothers World's Greatest Show had been growing and expanding by leaps and bounds, and was breathing down James A. Bailey's neck. It will be noted that the Ringlings had not hesitated to take the Barnum and Bailey title, change it around slightly, and apply it to themselves.

Then, one by one, the Ringlings began to absorb their rivals. Upon Bailey's death, they bought Barnum and Bailey and created the Big One—as they called the Combined Ringling Brothers and Barnum & Bailey Shows. The sale price was only $410,000. During their first combined season, they made a bigger profit than the Greatest Show on Earth had cost them.

In 1929, as the last surviving Ringling brother, John bought the American Circus Corporation for two million dollars. It consisted of some of the best-known shows in the country—

including Sells-Floto, Sparks, Hagenbeck-Wallace, Al G. Barnes, and John Robinson. Among them they owned 150 railroad cars, more than 2000 animals, 4500 performers, and incalculable amounts of tents, wagons, and other equipment.

At this time John was an extremely wealthy man. He had speculated successfully in oil ventures, real estate, and railroads. His total assets were estimated to be over fifty million dollars.

A few years before, he had visited the little Gulf Coast town of Sarasota, Florida, and had fallen in love with its peaceful charm. He built a vast, ornate mansion there, which he called Ca'd'Zan, meaning House of John in the dialect of Venice, Italy. He filled it with millions of dollars' worth of fine art treasures which he bought on his yearly trips to Europe in search of new talent for the show. Over the ensuing years, he persuaded the rest of the Ringling family to move to Sarasota. And eventually, in 1927, he moved the show's winter quarters to Sarasota from Bridgeport, Connecticut, where it had been since Barnum's time. He also built a Museum of the American Circus. Upon his death, he willed the house, the art collection, and the museum to the state of Florida. Thousands of people visit it every year—and Sarasota is known as the Circus City.

John Ringling lived like an oriental prince at Ca'd'Zan. He entertained, with a lavish hand, royalty from Europe, stars from Broadway and Hollywood, and leading figures in the world of sports. During the winter season, when he was not on the road with his show, it was always "open house" at the big mansion. Often he gave elaborate lawn parties to which he invited the entire population of Sarasota. (It was a small farming town then, and not the big resort and retirement city it has since become.) On Sundays, the circus band gave concerts for the public.

Then, when the New York stock market collapsed on
a bleak October day in 1929, John Ringling's circus empire began to collapse with it. He had millions of dollars
in assets, but very little in actual cash. He had borrowed
heavily to buy the American Circus Corporation only a few
months before. And when he was unable to pay his notes
promptly, the banks took over. For the few remaining years
of his life, he had to stand helplessly on the side lines
while other people ran the circus which had been born in
the youthful dreams of himself and his brothers that day
on the riverside wharf in McGregor.

John, the last of the brothers, died on December 2, 1936.
His estates and tied-up assets were listed at somewhat more
than $23 million, but there was just $311 in his personal
bank account.

For ten years after John's death, the Big One was in
continuous financial and managerial difficulties. The various
heirs of the original brothers were at constant odds. But
somehow the show managed to hit the rails every spring in
all its splendor.

Then another disaster struck. It was during the matinee
performance on July 6, 1944, at Hartford, Connecticut. The
big top was packed with men, women, and children who
were enjoying a long Fourth of July holiday weekend. Suddenly, in the middle of the show, smoke began to curl and
billow from the broad roof of the tent. Merle Evans, who
had been the circus band leader for thirty years—swung
his musicians into the strident strains of "The Stars and
Stripes Forever," a tune which is never played at the circus
except as a signal of disaster. High-wire acrobats slid down
ropes to the ground. The ringmaster stepped to the microphone and asked the crowd to leave quickly in an orderly
manner. Every employee of the circus—performers, clowns,

animal men, acrobats, roustabouts—began guiding the spectators to safety.

But within minutes, the whole of the big top was a roaring, flaming inferno. The crowd panicked and began a mad rush for the exits, trampling over each other in their stampede to the outdoors. Then the tent poles collapsed and the burning big top caved in. In ten minutes it was all over. The main tent was a heap of black ashes, covering the bodies of the dead and injured.

It was a miracle, considering the swiftness with which the whole catastrophe happened, and the thousands who were watching the show, that more people were not killed. When the final count was made, 186 people had died, more than half of them children, and 487 were severely burned. The circus itself was virtually a total loss.

Over the next few years, the Ringling management paid out more than five million dollars in damages. It is a tribute to the reputation of the Big One that it was able to rise like the mythical phoenix from the ashes and take to the road the next season.

Two years later, the heirs of all the Ringlings managed to settle their differences, and John Ringling North—old John's nephew and protégé—was made president of the circus corporation. North began at once to bring the show back to its former glory.

In 1956, John North abandoned canvas tents and began to play only in indoor arenas and ball parks. A few years later, the ball parks too were eliminated from the booking schedule and the circus was shown entirely indoors—in big amphitheaters such as New York's Madison Square Garden, Chicago's International Amphitheater, the Boston Garden, and the Houston Astrodome.

At last, in 1967, the Ringling family sold their circus after nearly a century of ownership. The reported price was in excess of ten million dollars. And two years after that, the Ringling Brothers and Barnum & Bailey Circus was split into two units, the Red Show and the Blue Show—both equal in size and both equally Stupendous! Gigantic! Colossal! Each unit plays a different section of the country, changing routes each alternate season. Currently the Big One is seen every summer in more than a hundred American cities.

A writer recently asked the new general manager of the circus a question:

"Of the two Ringling Brothers and Barnum & Bailey Circuses, which one is *really* the Greatest Show on Earth?"

The manager puffed thoughtfully on his cigar for a moment and then typically replied:

"They *both* are!"

Display #8

THE SAWDUST TRAILS

SOMEBODY once said that trying to figure out an exact chronological history of the early circus in America would be like attempting to unravel the geneology of the Jones family. There were so many little wagon shows slogging along the rural roads during the last half of the nineteenth century and the first part of the twentieth, that it would be an impossible task to keep an accurate track of them all.

But out of the hundreds of small and medium-sized circuses that crisscrossed the country in those days, bringing farmers and small-town people their one day of entertainment every year, a few fabulous figures emerged. Aside from Barnum, Bailey, and the brothers Ringling, some of the most colorful were Adam Forepaugh, the Sells brothers, Jerry Mugivan, Bert Bowers, Ed Ballard, Fred Bonfils, Harry Tammen—and ridiculously enough in that day of ridiculous goings-on, a sports writer named Otto Floto, who had nothing whatever to do with the circus except to lend his odd-sounding name to one of them.

The story of Adam Forepaugh reads as though it might have been written by Horatio Alger. It was a rags-to-riches saga in the classic sense of the word.

Unlike Barnum, Bailey, and the Ringlings, Forepaugh got into the circus game by accident, and was a phenomenal success at the age of thirty. He was a superb businessman and was probably the toughest competitor ever seen on the circus circuit. His rivals claimed that he squeezed every dollar that came his way so hard that the eagle screamed in agony. And to an extent this was true. He paid his performers and his hired help as little as he could get away with. But he spent money hand over fist for his menagerie—for which he sent his agents scouring all over the world—and his star acts were always offered top salaries to lure them away from other circus owners. Yet underneath his gruff, tightfisted exterior he possessed a unique sort of softheartedness. Whenever he saw a crippled person on the lot, he admitted him into the show free. And it is said that when he spied a small boy trying to sneak in under the edge of the tent—especially if the boy looked as though he really did not have the price of a ticket—he lifted up the canvas and shoved the kid inside.

Old Adam, as he was known to the circus fraternity, had a great love for animals—so much so that he often signed his ads and posters with the pun "4-Paw." This is understandable since he had made his original fortune by trading in horses.

Born Adam Vorback, in 1831, he quit school after getting just enough "book larnin'" to read, write, and, most importantly, add up figures in a ledger. He then went to work as a butcher's helper and errand boy. By the time he was eighteen, he owned his own butcher shop in Philadelphia. As a side line, he began to deal in horses. Within a year or two, he had made so much money as a horse trader that he gave up his butcher shop to devote all his time and energies to the much more lucrative commodity of live horseflesh.

In 1854, when the owner of a small and obscure wagon show called the Tom King Excelsior Circus was unable to pay for a string of horses, young Mr. Vorback took a half ownership in the show as payment. He soon bought out his

partner, changed his name and that of the circus to Forepaugh, and his star in the circus firmament began to shoot
up like a runaway rocket.

By the end of the Civil War, Forepaugh was operating
the biggest circus and menagerie in America. Until Barnum
came on the scene in 1871, he had no major competition. And when the Great Man finally did take out his show,
Old Adam gave him a rough and tumble run for his
money.

When Jumbo was the idol of the circus-going public,
Forepaugh plastered up posters announcing that both Barnum and Jumbo were frauds; and that his own star pachyderm, Bolivar, was actually the "largest and heaviest elephant in the world." His trick of whitewashing Old John as
a rival to Barnum's genuine Burmese white elephant—and
then billing him as being "Too White for Barnum"—was a
typical 4-Paw ploy.

Forepaugh was the most free-swinging name caller in
circus history. In his famous "wars" with Barnum, he displayed a no-holds-barred knack for writing insulting advertising copy that today could land a man in the libel courts.

When Barnum covered a town with posters advertising:

20 ELEPHANTS—100 ANIMAL CAGES—HUNDREDS OF
LADIES AND GENTLEMEN IN MILITARY AND CIVILIAN
COSTUMES. . . . (etc.)

Forepaugh hastily booked his own show into the same town
for a week or so later and put up his own posters which
typically read:

A BUBBLE PRICKED! SOLD AGAIN!

Then, listing all Barnum's promises of wonders to be seen
at the Greatest Show on Earth, Old Adam's posters went
on:

EVERY STATEMENT MADE ABOVE IS A
GROSS EXAGGERATION!
WITHOUT A SINGLE WORD OF TRUTH!
WAIT FOR THE OLD RELIABLE
FOREPAUGH SHOW!
THE LARGEST SHOW IN THE WORLD!
WHICH EXPOSES
FRAUD! FALSEHOOD! AND DOWNRIGHT DECEIT!
IN THE INTERESTS OF THE PEOPLE!

Barnum's advance men hurriedly ran off posters and newspaper ads which were just as ludicrous, lashing back at the Forepaugh Show.

These insulting, name-calling, small-boyish rival posters were commonplace among almost all early circuses; but Forepaugh and Barnum carried them to extremes. They have become famous in circus lore as "rat bills" and original copies today are collectors' items.

After a few years of such fierce and virulent competition, which proved to be more costly than worthwhile to both men, Forepaugh and Barnum agreed on an armed truce. They divided up the country between them, alternating each year between the Eastern and Western states. Indeed, one year they combined their shows for a grand double opener in New York, and then went their separate ways for the remainder of the season.

When Forepaugh died suddenly in 1890, the "Old Reliable Forepaugh Show" died with him.

Fifteen years later, James A. Bailey bought the name, joined it with that of the defunct Sells brothers show to form the Forepaugh-Sells Circus, and put it on the road under an independent management. But without Old Adam at the controls, it was never the same again. After one year, Bailey in turn sold it to the Ringlings—and a season or so later it quietly folded.

Except for the Ringlings, the most famous circus-family team was that of the brothers Sells—Eph, Ad, Lewis, and Peter. Begun in 1871, the Sells Brothers Circus and Menagerie was owned and operated by the family until 1905.

As did most of the early circuses, the show sprouted up haphazardly. Ad had started out with a little one-horse "hippodrome." But before the first season was completed, his brothers became enamored with the glamor of the sawdust trail, sold out their business in Ohio, and joined him. Gradually they acquired some rolling stock and sundry animals that they picked up here and there from small, nondescript shows which had "gone bust" on the road.

By 1878, they had done so well that they were able to buy three or four other small circuses in their entirety. That spring they took to the rails in thirty-two cars, billed as Sells Brothers Great European Seven Elephant Railroad Show. The "seven elephant" reference was a knock at Barnum, who that year had a herd of only six.

Remember, the more elephants you could claim, the bigger and better your circus was supposed to be.

The Sells brothers informally, and with the correct proportion of country corn, labeled their circus the "corn and wheat belt show," and traveled mainly through the Middle West. They scheduled their bookings with a weather eye out for those sections of the prairie land that were enjoying the most favorable crop years, and therefore had the most loose money to spend. After ten years or so of growing prosperity, their circus was large enough and well known enough to become a serious rival to Barnum and Forepaugh.

But a couple of decades later the Sells Circus finally came to grief when the soaring success of Barnum and Bailey and the rising star of the Ringlings slowly but surely began to squeeze it out of business. In 1905, the last brother, Lewis, sold out to James A. Bailey, who incorporated the circus into the Forepaugh-Sells Circus—and the following year sold it to the Ringlings.

And so another great old-timer bit the dust.

The Sells name came alive again briefly a year later in one of the zaniest wheeling-dealing maneuvers in all the zany annals of the big top.

Fred Bonfils and Harry Tammen were two harum-scarum newspaper publishers in Denver, Colorado. Their paper, the Denver *Post,* was practically a three-ring circus in itself. They specialized in screaming headlines and muck-raking scandals. On their particular whim of the moment they crusaded for—or just as often against—almost everything from shoot-outs in the city streets, to the Spanish-American War, the local streetcar company, and the President of the United States. Starting with next to nothing, they had built the *Post* into a multi-million-dollar operation and the most powerful newspaper in the West.

In 1902, looking around for something new to play with, Tammen bought a down-at-the-heels dog and pony show that had gone broke in Denver. A dog and pony show in those days was precisely what the name implied. It consisted solely of trained dogs and ponies, with possibly a mediocre clown or two cavorting between the acts.

The publisher wanted an eye-catching name for his first venture into the circus world, so he christened it the Floto Dog and Pony Show, naming it after Otto Floto, the sports editor of the *Post.* Floto owned no part of the fledgling circus, nor did he ever have anything to do with the ownership or management of any of Bonfils and Tammen's subsequent sawdust enterprises. But Tammen was enchanted by the name Floto—which was why he had hired the sports writer in the first place—and he was sure that it would be an extra-added box office attraction.

Over the following few years, as the *Post* partners poured money into their show, it grew to the dimensions of a full-sized circus—with a large menagerie, a dozen elephants, acrobatic acts, trained animals, and top-notch clowns. By 1906, Tammen and Bonfils decided that their presentation was now too big and grandiose to be called simply a dog and pony show. So they looked around for a well-known name that would give it some class and stature.

It so happened that old Ad Sells had had an adopted son named Willie, who was then out of work. Tammen hired him as assistant manager, gave him two or three shares of stock to qualify him as a part owner, and retitled the show the Sells-Floto Circus. With his usual flair for publicity values, and his disdain for the strict truth, Tammen put pictures of all four of the Sells brothers, as well as that of Otto Floto, on his billboards and posters.

The Ringling brothers, who by this time owned the original Sells Brothers Circus, hit the ceiling of their ticket wagon. They immediately sued Bonfils and Tammen for two million dollars. But for once the brothers from Baraboo had stuck their heads into a hornet's nest. The Denver *Post* was very nearly all-powerful in the Rocky Mountain country, and Bonfils and Tammen aimed their editorial big guns squarely at the Ringlings. They called Ringling Brothers and Barnum & Bailey "the circus trust." Whenever the Big One booked into a town and put up posters to announce their forthcoming show, Sells-Floto advance men covered up the Ringling three-sheets with posters of their own.

The Ringlings retaliated by pasting up signs over the Sells-Floto posters that proclaimed: RINGLING BROTH-

ERS COMING SOON! The *Post* began derisively to call Ringling Brothers the "Coming Soon Circus."

Bonfils and Tammen had made it their business over the years to find out where a good many political bodies were buried. And so great was their influence that not only did the two-million-dollar damage suit come to nothing, but they managed to get local licensing fees boosted up so exorbitantly high that the Ringlings were prevented from showing in Denver and several other Western cities.

As if that wasn't enough, the Denver circus men began raiding the Ringlings' talent. Without increasing ther salaries, they succeeded in hiring away some of the best acrobats, riders, and clowns.

In his book *Timber Line,* Gene Fowler, who was then a cub reporter on the *Post,* revealed Tammen's secret for this remarkable feat. He quoted Tammen, roughly and somewhat edited, about as follows:

"You see," Tammen explained, "money or no money, the one thing you've got to do is provide the best cook-tent in the world. All men love their stomachs—rich, poor, white, black, acrobats, clowns, and Supreme Court justices. If we get the best cook-tent, we'll get the best performers. They'll say, 'It's a good show, but the cook-tent is the greatest.'"

When the truth served Mr. Tammen's turn, he at least met it halfway. He modestly billed his Sells-Floto Circus as "The *Second* Greatest Show on Earth."

Harry Tammen was fascinated by elephants. But as they were for so many other circus owners, his bulls were a constant source of headaches. During one matinee performance in a Southern California town, the menagerie tent caught on fire. Four of the prize bulls—Alice, Freida, Old Snyder, and Floto—broke loose from their leg chains, knocked over animal cages, shattered the tent poles, scared the daylights out of the customers, and scattered over the sunny orangegroved countryside. Fred Alispaw, the manager of the menagerie, hastily organized a sort of mounted posse of roustabouts, police, and firemen and gave chase.

Freida got herself bogged down in a clay bank and was easily captured. Old Snyder wrecked an orange grove, uprooted a few dozen trees, and was happily eating the fruit when his pursuers caught up with him. Alice descended on a chicken farm and got herself so thoroughly tangled up in chicken wire that she couldn't move. But Floto caused the real trouble.

He charged a farmhouse, demolished the front porch, and squashed an old lady to death who was sitting there sunning herself. When the posse cornered him, the smack of rifle bullets against his pachydermous hide only infuriated him further. He crashed through the front of a small hotel and then on out the back, carrying a portion of the wall festooned around his neck like a Hawaiian lei. He then smashed through the side of a livery stable, where Alispaw at last managed to subdue him.

Tammen got off easy. He paid total damages for the afternoon's elephantine frolic of only seventeen thousand dollars.

A year or so later, Alice gave birth to a baby son. Old Snyder was the proud father, but Alice was anything but a proud mother. Her first act after the baby was born was to sit down on him and try to smash him to death. Alispaw and his bull-men succeeded in rescuing the bewildered, terrified, and half-dead calf and nursed him back to life on a diet of cow's milk laced with whisky.

Tammen was an even prouder father than Old Snyder. With a fine disregard for Bailey's Young America, who had been born some thirty years before, Tammen elaborately billed the little fellow as "the first elephant ever born in America." He named it Little Hutch and charged an extra admission to view it in the menagerie tent. For the street parades, Alice pushed him in an out-sized baby carrage. Little Hutch earned a thousand dollars a day for his owners until his death at the tender age of two months.

Two years later, Alice calved another son. For this momentous event, and with much blaring of publicity trumpets, Tammen imported a team of veterinarians from as far away as the Central Park Zoo in New York. But as she had done with Little Hutch, Alice tried to kill him a moment after he was born. When he was saved from the insane wrath of his mother, Tammen was jubilant and made great plans for the infant. But this second baby, called Tambon after Tammen and Bonfils, survived for less than a month.

Strangely enough, for it has never happened since, Alice had two more male calves in the next few years. Again, she attempted to squash them both as soon as they were born, and both of them lived only a few weeks.

After the death of his fourth son, Old Snyder became completely insane and unmanageable. Maybe it was because he despaired of ever having an heir—for who knows what goes on in an elephant's tiny brain. In any case, Tammen and Alispaw sentenced him to death in the interest of all-around safety, and he is reported to have given one final defiant trumpet call as the high-powered rifle bullets of his executioners ended his life.

Tammen at last sold Alice to the zoo in Salt Lake City. She was paid for with pennies, nickels, and dimes contributed by Utah school children. There she lived out a long and placid life, safely secured behind iron bars.

Tammen and Bonfils liked to bill big names on their show. They hired both Jess Williard and Jack Dempsey when each was the heavyweight boxing champion of the world. And they deliberately threw the fabulous Buffalo Bill Wild West

Show into bankruptcy so they could then hire Bill Cody back under their own banner.

In 1920, after eighteen years of traveling the sawdust trail, both Tammen and Bonfils became bored with their three-ring plaything and sold it to the American Circus Corporation—which later was bought by John Ringling.

But the Sells-Floto shenanigans had been a barrel of fun—along with a good deal of assorted grief—for all concerned.

The American Circus Corporation was a sawdust octopus. It was formed about 1920 by three free-wheeling promoters named Jerry Mugivan, Bert Bowers, and Ed Ballard. By the time they finally sold it outright to John Ringling, they had managed to take over just about every popular circus property in the United States with the notable exception of the Ringling enterprise.

During the opening years of the 1900s, the circus business was a confusing mishmash. Much of its chronology sounds like pure guesswork. Shows changed their names from season to season, switched ownerships, were forced to the wall by stronger rivals, bought up, sold at auction, and in general juggled like so many tarnished tinsel balls in the air.

Among the famous-name circuses that Mugivan, Bowers, and Ballard swallowed up were Dode Fiske, Dan Robinson, the Great Van Amburgh Shows, Howes' Great London Circus, Sells-Floto, John Robinson, John H. Sparks, Al G. Barnes, and Hagenbeck-Wallace.

Carl Hagenbeck was an animal trainer from Hamburg, Germany, who had exhibited his wild beasts all over Europe, and later helped found the famous Hamburg Zoo. He originated the idea of rewarding his animals with a tidbit of their favorite food after a successful trick, a practice that is used by all trainers today. This makes a lion or a tiger no less dangerous to handle—but only a little more willing to cooperate in something that his natural instincts tell him not to do in the first place.

In 1906, Hagenbeck brought his animal acts to this country and formed a short-lived partnership with a veteran circus man named Ben Wallace.

Until Hagenbeck's arrival on the American circus scene, wild animals had been exhibited in their small traveling cages. It was his idea to construct a large arena-like cage in the circus's center ring in which the trainer could put his animals through their paces, as is now done in all modern shows.

After only a year, Hagenbeck sold out his interest to Wallace, who carried on alone—but still under the Hagenbeck-Wallace name—until he was forced to bow to the big circus trust.

By 1929, very few small independent circuses were left. Chiefly they were ragtag shows that moved from place to place in trucks instead of railroad cars. They played the little towns and villages that were uneconomic stands for the big boys. They had a few clowns, a cage or two of animals, some trick riders, a handful of third-rate acrobats and wire-walkers, and maybe a glued-together Wild West show.

But in the rural back country areas of America, such a fly-by-night circus was better than no circus at all.

Display #9

THE WILD AND WOOLLY WEST

I N THE make believe wonderland world of the big top, William Frederick "Buffalo Bill" Cody was the real thing.

He was the living symbol of adventure and derring-do to a generation of Americans. He was bigger than big, the boy who never grew up, the All-American hero. His Indian name was Pahaska, meaning Long Hair, for his thick brown locks swept triumphantly down over the shoulders of his beaded buckskin jacket. He could knock over a jack rabbit at fifty feet with either a rifle or a six-shooter. When he galloped out into the arena on his milk-white stallion to open his Wild West Show, he was, as one biographer described him, "the finest figure of a horseman who ever lived." He was the last of the six great scouts of the American frontier—Boone, Bridger, Hickok, Carson, Crockett, and Cody.

Bill shot and killed his first Indian at the age of twelve, when a Sioux war party attacked a wagon train on which he was working as an odd-jobs hand. When he was fourteen, he was the youngest rider on the fabled Pony Express. This was a sort of Herculean horse race in which relays of riders carried the mail at a dead run over the two-thousand-mile route from St. Joseph, Missouri, to Sacramento, California— mostly through country infested by hostile Indians and highwaymen—in the unheard-of time of nine days.

The Pony Express came to an abrupt end when the first

transcontinental telegraph line was completed in 1861. By
this time the Civil War had begun. Bill added a couple of
years to his age and joined the Union Army. He served
mostly as a scout on the Western frontier.

Immediately upon the heels of Lee's surrender at Ap-
pomattox came the great railroad boom. Bill Cody signed on
as a professional buffalo hunter for the Kansas-Pacific Railroad, which was laying a segment of the coast-to-coast track.

In those days of the wide-open spaces, millions of buffaloes
covered the vast prairie lands like a broad moving carpet
of brown. The Kansas-Pacific employed more than twelve
hundred section hands, which meant that they needed tons of
fresh meat every week. In one season, Bill killed a record
4862 of the great beasts. It was this kind of reckless
slaughter that very nearly made the American bison as
extinct as the dodo bird or the passenger pigeon. By 1905,
when the first animal conservation law was passed by Congress, there were only about one hundred of the splendid
animals left in the whole of North America. (The herds
have now been rebuilt and are kept on reservations.)

But in the late 1860s, the supply seemed inexhaustible.
And to Bill Cody buffalo hunting was just a job—a job that
was destined to give him a nickname by which he would be
affectionately known to millions of hero-worshipers for the
rest of his life. Buffalo Bill!

When the railroad was finished, Bill was appointed Chief
of Scouts for General Wesley Merritt's Fifth Cavalry, a
unit of the United States Army which had been assigned to
put down the uprising of the Plains Indians during the
middle seventies.

One day in July of 1876, near a little stream called
Warbonnet Creek on the edge of the Dakota Territory, the
Fifth accidentally bumped into an Indian army of about
two thousand Sioux and Cheyenne warriors under the com-

mand of a chief named Yellow Hand. This was a part of the big Indian force that had wiped out General George Custer's Seventh Regiment to the last man at the battle of the Little Bighorn only a week or so before. Merritt's command was badly outnumbered.

As the soldiers took up defensive positions, they were amazed to see a lone Indian race his pony out into the open area between the two opposing forces, brandishing his repeating rifle over his head. He was a big man, riding a big pinto. His face was fiercely streaked with war paint, and an elaborate war bonnet of eagle feathers flowed down over his back and flapped in the breeze. As he rode up and down the line, he shouted out in a loud defiant voice that he, Yellow Hand, greatest of the Cheyenne, challenged Pahaska, bravest of the palefaces, to a personal combat.

Bill yelled, "That suits me fine!" and put a spur to his horse. There was a great whoop from the mass of Indians, and Bill's comrades set up a cheer.

At a distance of about thirty yards, both men fired their guns. Bill's shot killed Yellow Hand's pony, but at the same instant his horse stepped into a gopher hole and went down. Both fighters rolled over, neither seriously hurt, and scrambled to their feet. Each had managed to hold on to his rifle.

As Bill told the story many years later:

"We were now on foot and not more than twenty paces apart. We fired at each other simultaneously. My usual luck did not desert me on this occasion, for his bullet went wide of its mark while mine struck him squarely in the chest. He reeled and fell, but before he was fairly on the ground I was upon him, knife in hand, and drove the weapon hilt-deep into his heart. Then, I regret to say, I jerked off his war bonnet and scientifically scalped him."

"That was a bloodthirsty thing to do," said the newspaperman to whom Bill was telling the tale.

"Yes," Bill agreed, "but Custer had been my good friend and I wanted revenge. I sent the scalp to my wife, and when she saw what it was she fainted."

With their chief dead, the Indians retreated and disappeared into the hills.

It was this fight that made Bill Cody world famous. A writer named Ned Buntline was touring the Western frontier in search of ideas for adventure stories. When he heard of the duel at Warbonnet Creek he looked Bill up, saw at a glance that he was the perfect prototype of the Western frontiersman, and wrote a series of thrillers—called "dime novels" in those days—in which he made "Buffalo Bill" the hero. All of them were completely fictional, or at least highly exaggerated. But it wasn't long before almost everyone in the United States knew Bill's name.

After that, it was just one step from the sagebrush to the stage. Buntline's books were made into melodramatic plays in which Bill took the leading roles. With his resonant voice, his tall, broad-shouldered good looks, and his long hair, he was a natural matinee idol. Over the next several years, he played theaters from one end of the country to the other.

Then he got his great idea.

The people of the East knew very little about the great West that Bill loved so well. So, he decided, if Easterners couldn't come out to see the West, he would take the West to them. Not on a stage, but in an outdoor arena—complete with cowboys, Indians, scouts, buffaloes, and bucking horses.

Bill stewed over the idea of a Western show for more than a year. Then the people of North Platte, Nebraska, Bill's home town, handed his show to him all wrapped up in a neat package. They asked him to organize their Fourth of July and Frontier Day celebration. They wanted bronc busters, ropers, trick shooting—a real live Western rodeo. Local ranchers drove in herds of horses and cattle, and local cow-boys furnished the talent. The show was a glorious success. And when it was over, Bill realized that he had almost exactly the kind of show on his hands that he had been dreaming about. He started at once to enlarge and re-organize it. He sent messages to all his old friends on the frontier, and got down to serious work.

A herd of buffaloes was rounded up on the plains, along with a hundred or so longhorn steers. All of the top riders, ropers, and expert shots—as well as many of his old com-panions from the Pony Express—were eager to join up. He arranged to have friendly Indians brought in from the reservations. The Army, mindful of Bill's long service, and also conscious of the publicity value the show would bring with it, gave squadrons of crack cavalry special leave.

One of the prize exhibits was the famous old Deadwood Stage Coach, which had been on regular runs through the West for more than twenty years and had survived dozens of attacks by Indians and holdup men. On one notable oc-casion, when the stage was hauling a load of gold from the mines, it was waylaid by bandits and the driver was killed. A woman passenger named Martha Jane Canary—better known in Western lore as Calamity Jane—dodged the hail of flying bullets, jumped into the driver's seat, whipped up the horses, and took the coach safely away. Bill had the old stage refurbished and refitted.

Bill called his show the Wild West, Rocky Mountain and Prairie Exhibition. It opened in Omaha on May 17, 1883. The show met with such an enthusiastic reception that Bill felt justified in putting it on the rails and taking it on a nationwide tour. During the first few seasons it played outdoors, chiefly in county fairgrounds. Later it went under canvas. It was not a circus in the strictest sense of the word. There were no wild animals—except the buffaloes, the half-wild cattle, and the bucking horses—no freaks, no acrobats, no clowns. But it was one of the most spine-tingling shows that Americans had ever seen, and customers' eyes popped at the wild and woolly goings-on.

Indian braves, decked out in war paint and head feathers, raced their ponies around the big circular track and filled the air with frightful war whoops. The cavalry went through mounted drills at a dead run. Cowboys herded droves of cattle and buffaloes, rode outlaw horses, performed fancy roping and shooting tricks. The Pony Express riders demonstrated how they had carried the mail in the pre-telegraph and pre-railroad days. A covered wagon was attacked by Indians and rescued by a squad of soldiers. The Deadwood Coach was held up by highwaymen and saved by Buffalo Bill and a band of frontier scouts.

Bill himself was, of course, the star of the show. Riding at top speed he broke small glass balls—which were tossed into the air by a horseman who rode ahead of him—with his rifle and six-shooter. And he could always create a wild round of cheers and applause simply by loping around the ring on his big white horse, waving his ten-gallon hat, and taking deep bows from the saddle.

Some years before, Bill had adopted an orphan boy, Johnny Baker, whom he taught to ride and shoot. Later he was joined by the celebrated Annie Oakley, "Little Sure Shot," a young girl from Ohio who was probably the greatest female sharpshooter of all time.

In none of these shooting exhibitions were solid cartridges used. Instead the marksmen loaded their guns with small, relatively low-power scatter-shot that made a small pattern as it expanded. The effect was just as dramatic. This is not to say that Bill or Annie or Johnny could not have hit their targets with high-powered rifle or pistol bullets. It would simply have been taking unnecessary risks in the big crowds that packed the show at every performance.

During the next two years, Buffalo Bill's Wild West played to millions of people in cities and towns from San Francisco to New York and Boston. And the performers were no less colorful off-stage than on. They were authentic Westerners, rough, tough, and rowdy. Whenever they hit a city they whooped it up, just as they had been used to doing in small cow towns at the end of a cattle drive. They headed for the nearest saloon where the delighted bartender usually served them drinks on the house. Sometimes these celebrations went on until well past daybreak. And on more than one occasion, when it came time for the afternoon performance, it was all they could do to keep from falling off their horses. As often as not, Bill Cody whooped it up right along with them.

In addition to the West's top cowboys and horse wranglers, Bill persuaded some of the best-known Indian chiefs to tour with his show. One season he managed to engage his old arch-enemy Sitting Bull, who had master-minded the Custer massacre at the Little Bighorn River. Bill Cody had done his share of Indian fighting and had killed his share of hostiles, but he always had a healthy respect for the red man. Back on the frontier, as a scout, he had counseled the army generals: "The whole secret of dealing with Indians is to be honest with them and, above all, keep your word." For the most part the generals and Indian agents had ignored this sage advice. But Bill applied that principle scrupulously when he hired Indians for his Wild West Show. They all had a great respect for the fearless Pahaska. And the cowboys did too. Anything they could do, Bill could do better.

During the next twenty years, Buffalo Bill Cody was the most admired American of his time. He was a personal friend of presidents and kings. The governor of Nebraska made him an honorary colonel of the state militia. Whenever he walked down the streets of a city, crowds gathered to shake his hand. He always wore diamond cuff links and a diamond tiepin, shaped like the head of a buffalo, which were given to him by the Grand Duke Alexis of Russia, whom he had once guided on a buffalo hunt. He spent money as though it came pouring from a bottomless cornucopia. And, in the end, he died broke.

For several seasons Bill took his show to London and Paris, where it always played to sellout houses. At a Command Performance for Queen Victoria, the kings of Denmark, Saxony, Belgium, and Greece rode as passengers in the Deadwood Stage—while the Prince of Wales, later to become King Edward VII of England, sat on the box next to Bill and the driver.

"Did you ever hold four kings before?" the young prince asked after the show.

"Many times," Bill came right back. "But never four kings and a joker."

To open every show, Bill rode out into the arena alone, swept off his hat, and made an elegant bow. As he grew older, Bill's hair turned white and began to get thin on top. Somebody suggested that he wear a toupee. The first time he wore his new toupee, it came off with the hat. But such was the public's admiration for the man that there was not a single titter from the audience. Bill never wore the wig again.

Buffalo Bill Cody was a superlative showman, but he was a poor businessman. He earned millions. But like so many big top immortals, he squandered it as fast as it came in. He never failed to pick up a check for food or drink no matter how many dozens—or hundreds—of people were present. He built churches, parks, and fairgrounds in his native state of Nebraska. He was always a soft touch for any old friend who might be down on his luck. His many investments, which he usually made on a sentimental hunch, began to go bad. He lost his ranch in Nebraska, his hotel in Cody, Wyoming, and, eventually, all his other real estate and mining ventures.

During his long show business career, which spanned more than a quarter of a century, Bill had many partners and business managers—including James A. Bailey, P. T. Barnum's old sidekick. At the height of his popularity, the Wild West Show made him a fortune. But in his later years, he saw his riches slip away. In 1913, he was teamed up with Major Gordon W. (Pawnee Bill) Lillie in what was called the Buffalo Bill Wild West and Pawnee Bill Great Far East Show. The show collapsed in mid-season for lack of operating capital, and Bill applied to Fred Bonfils and Harry Tammen, publishers of the Denver *Post,* for a loan.

This was what Bonfils and Tammen had been waiting for. They wanted Bill's name and reputation for their Sells-Floto Circus. When his note became due and Bill could not pay, the publishers sold him out for debt, and then hired him as an attraction for their own show.

Buffalo Bill Cody was becoming an old man. His health was rapidly failing, but his pride was big as ever; and his fight to keep that pride was a tougher one than any he'd ever had with hostile Indians on the Great Plains. He never missed opening the show with his usual flourish, galloping around the ring and shooting glass balls from the saddle. Sometimes he was so ill that he could hardly sit his horse. And sometimes, it must be admitted, he was suffering from too ample a medication of bourbon and branch water.

Buffalo Bill died in 1917, and he lies buried in a magnificent tomb which was blasted out of the solid granite of Lookout Mountain, on a peak of the Rockies high above Denver. With him died the Wild West Show that had been the child of his own genius and imagination. A lot of imitations followed him, but none had the Cody magic.

To name only a few, there were the 101 Ranch Show, Young Buffalo Bill's Wild West, Buckskin Bill's Wild West, and Kit Carson's Wild West. After Cody's death, Pawnee Bill Lillie attempted a comeback, but failed in less than a season. Frank James (Jesse's brother) and Cole Younger, both of them notorious outlaws and train robbers, had the nerve to take a show on the road and hope that nobody arrested them. The show folded before any lawman could catch up with them. Old silent movie cowboy stars—Tom Mix, Tim McCoy, Ken Maynard, and Buck Jones—all put Western shows together, but none of them were successful.

Still today almost all the small traveling circuses that play rural small towns put on an after-show, or "concert" —for which an extra admission fee is charged—that is a sort of Wild West Show. But all of them are pale parodies of Bill Cody's great pageantry.

When William Frederick Cody made his final exit from the circus scene, the Wild and Woolly West followed him to the egress.

Display #10

STREET PARADES AND SIDE SHOWS

Two classic features of the American circus, both of which in the old days were almost as thrilling as the big show itself, have passed from the sawdust scene. One was the pre-show street parade, and the other the ubiquitous side show.

The parade, of course, had its remote beginnings in ancient Rome. But it is doubtful if Barnum or Forepaugh or the Ringlings had ever heard of these Roman spectacles. To them, the parade was a come-on, a sampling of the goodies that were awaiting under the big top.

The first street parade in the United States, according to historian Marian Murray, was a hastily put-together affair staged by a small and long-forgotten circus named Purdy, Welch, McComber & Company, in Albany, New York, in the spring of 1837. To lure customers to their tent, they paraded a brass band down the main street of the town, with two drummers on elephants bringing up the rear.

From that humble beginning, the street parade expanded and grew. Owners were quick to sense that if townspeople got a free glimpse of elephants, caged animals, clowns, acrobats, colorful wagons, and bespangled horseback riders, they would then scurry out to the show ground and plunk down the price of admission.

Every circus parade was as elaborate as the owner could afford—for after all it was his showcase. Next to the herd of elephants, marching sedately along tail-in-trunk, the chief features of the street parades were the floats, the animal cages and—most of all—the bandwagons.

The floats depicted scenes out of mythology and fairy tales. The animal cages, especially those which contained snake charmers and their pets, were usually glass-sided. The larger shows carried up to a dozen or more of these so-called "dens." After the parade, the dens were displayed in the menagerie tent, and the snake charmers did their acts in the side shows.

But, above all, it was the bandwagons that were the true works of circus art. Ornately carved, brilliantly painted, covered with as much golden gilt as the show's budget could bear, they were usually pulled by hitches of from six to sixteen horses. In the bigger circuses, two or three brass bands, seated on top, filled the air with a blare of noise that could be heard for miles. Along with the bands, every circus had to have at least one steam calliope, which gave out an even more window-shaking blast than did the bands. When the parade went down the street, in all its ear-splitting, eye-popping glory, nobody could miss the fact that the circus had come to town. For several seasons, P. T. Barnum interrupted his parade at intervals to fire off twenty-one-gun salutes. The President of the United States was only officially entitled to eighteen. But Barnum made up his own rules as he went along.

The most glorious and famous of all the old-time band-wagons was the "Two Hemispheres," which was the star attraction of the Barnum and Bailey parade. A gold-colored bas-relief of the Western Hemisphere decorated one side of the wagon, and an equally fancy depiction of the Eastern side of the world covered the other. This enormous contraption was built in 1896 at a cost of forty thousand dollars and was pulled by forty horses, harnessed four abreast in a military hitch. It was driven by a man named Jake

Posey, who held twenty separate reins—one for each pair of horses—intertwined between the fingers of both hands.

One day in 1887 when James A. Bailey took the circus to England, the parade was proceeding grandly through the narrow, crooked streets of a small town in Norfolk called King's Lynn. Getting the forty-horse bandwagon around a corner was quite a feat, and Posey had developed a technique for doing so that required the most precise timing and dexterity. Since no whip was long enough to guide the maneuvers of two score horses, Posey had a helper on the driver's seat beside him who threw pebbles with a baseball pitcher's dead aim at whichever horse needed to be urged.

Posey's method of rounding corners was to have his lead horses take it at a run, so that the rest of the hitch would be around it before they all straightened out again, thus keeping the gigantic bandwagon from lurching up on the sidewalk.

On this particular day in King's Lynn, as Posey was rounding a corner in his customary fashion, a startled British bobby saw the great mass of horses bearing down upon him at a rapid clip. He leaped for the bridles of the lead horses, hauled them to an abrupt stop and thus threw the whole timing of the maneuver out of kilter. The following horses rammed into each other and the big bandwagon ran up over the curb, swerved into a pub, and took the whole front of it away.

Bailey paid for the damage, but the pub owner capitalized on the accident. He renamed his establishment the Forty-Horse Inn, and grew rich on the new prosperity that all the publicity had brought it.

It was not long before Bailey abandoned the street parade as a pre-show feature in Europe. The Europeans were unaware of American customs and thought that after the splendor of the parade there could not possibly be anything left worth paying to see, thus staying away from the main show in droves. But back in America Bailey quickly revived it, and on an ever increasing scale. For as far as the American public was concerned, a circus wasn't a circus unless it was preceded by a parade.

For many good reasons, the circus parade has long been a thing of the past. Chief among these is the fact that the streets of even the smallest cities in America have for thirty years or more been clogged with automobile traffic, and even a modest circus parade would bring business in any town to a congested halt.

Gone too, alas, with the winds of change are the blatant old bandwagons. Even the most elaborate and expensive of them have long since rotted away and fallen into ruin. The only ones still existing are those on display at museums in such circus-conscious towns as Sarasota and Baraboo.

Gone also are the days of the side show, which, like the parade, was a must at any circus.

From earliest times, and especially in nineteenth-century America when any kind of entertainment was at a premium, the exhibition of rarities—and most particularly human abnormalities—was a sure-fire come-on. The showing of freaks had its rude beginnings in the mountebank shows of the Middle Ages. P. T. Barnum built it to classic proportions in his New York Museum.

The side-show tent was always opened on the circus grounds two or three hours before the big show began so that early attendees would have plenty of time to spend their extra money for a look at the freaks and fakes. And all circus fans went early in order not to miss any of the wonders that were in store. A typical side show of a few years ago consisted of a giant, a midget or two, a fat man or woman, a bearded lady, a fire-eater, a sword swallower, a pretty young girl who allowed boa constrictors to coil themselves around her body, a tattooed man or woman, a man with no arms who signed autographs (at a dime a throw) by holding a pen between his toes, a strong man, a magician, a fortune-teller. You can just about name it, and the old-time side show had it. All these people performed on a long platform, and a master of ceremonies introduced each act in turn.

Most of the old-time circus freaks were horrifying to look at, and yet fascinating for the local yokels. The stunt performers, such as the fire-eaters and sword swallowers, were no less amazing; but their tricks were carefully practiced and perfected over the years.

Sword swallowers, for example, employed a well-studied knowledge of the human anatomy. When the face is tilted back at the proper angle, the throat and the esophagus tube make a straight line to the stomach. Depending upon a man's height, it is from twelve to eighteen inches long. With a great deal of training and practice, a man with steel nerves can pass a narrow object, such as the dull blade of a sword, down this straight opening. The greatest obstacle that has to be overcome, so a sword swallower once told me, is to learn to conquer the normal instinct to gag when a foreign object is inserted into the throat. Naturally, most sword swallowers cheated by using swords with retractable blades. Thus a sword blade which was to all outward appearances two or three feet long, could be retracted to a third of that length once it was in the performer's mouth.

Another breath-taking side-show trickster was the man who stuck pins into his eyes. A well-lubricated pin can be pushed an inch or two into the tear duct which is located at the eye's inner corner. (Certainly this is not a trick to be attempted unless one knows precisely what he is doing.) The performer then held open the eyelids with his fingers, rolled his eyeball, and the pin seemed to rotate with it—apparently as though it were indeed imbedded into the eye itself.

Still another eye-boggling trick was the man, usually dressed as an Indian fakir, who stuck pins into one cheek and out the other. This required a lot of preparation. The cheeks are not as closely threaded with nerves as are most other parts of the body. The trick was to discover, by trial and painful error, which part of the cheek a long pin could be inserted into. Then, by repeated insertions, the tiny wounds would heal leaving small holes through which the pin could be pushed with no pain at all. A similar trick could be performed by creating a hole in the tongue into which a pin could be stuck. Actually it was little different from the manner in which many women have their earlobes pierced for earrings.

Fire-eating, too, was the result of long and often painful practice. The fire-eater coated his mouth with a protective type of grease. He would then thrust a flaming torch of burning kerosene into his mouth, tightly compress his lips and blow outward against his cheeks so that the fire and hot air did not get into his lungs and nasal passages. After a second or two, he quickly pulled out the torch, still burning, and emitted a great cloud of smoke and flame from his mouth. The inside of every fire-eater's mouth was a mass of scar tissue, usually acquired when he was learning his trade. And not a few aspiring tyros were killed by inhaling the fiery gases. But running such risks was thought by these people to be better than working.

The list of bodily freaks in the old-time circuses was almost endless. Some of the most astounding—and most gruesome—were:

Jo Jo the Dog-faced Boy. Jo Jo was a Russian whose real name was Theodore Peteroff. His entire face—forehead, cheeks, ears, and nose—was completely covered by a long growth of silken hair. He was sometimes billed as the Human Skye Terrier.

Madam Josephine Clofullia, Barnum's original Bearded Lady, had a son named Esau who inherited his mother's hirsute proclivities. At the age of four he sported a fine full-faced beard. Barnum often exhibited mother and son as a double feature.

Francisco Lentini was the Italian who possessed three legs. Two were in their normal places, and the third grew out of the back of his spine. As a boy he used all three to walk and run; but as he grew older the extra leg failed to develop as did the other two. He appeared on the freak platform with both the Ringling and the Buffalo Bill shows.

Myrtle Corbin went Lentini one leg better. She had four—two normal ones which she used for walking, and two smaller ones that dangled down between them.

Jean Libbera, another Italian who was shown by the Barnum and Bailey Show, had what nature intended as a twin brother growing out of his navel. The parasitic twin, which Jean called Jacques, was small but perfectly formed. He had shoulders, arms, fingers, legs, and toes—but his head was inside his brother's stomach. Jean and Jacques shared the same blood stream and nervous system. If you touched Jacques, Jean could feel it. Amazingly enough Jean Libbera, like Chang and Eng, the famous Siamese twins, married a normal girl and was the father of four normal children.

Another fantastic pair of side-show twins were the brothers Toccis, from Turin. They had been born of normal parents and had nine normal brothers and sisters. Below the waist they were one person; above the waist they were two. They had two legs, one stomach, four arms, two chests, and two heads. In spite of this monstrous physical condition, they were bright intelligent boys who developed into fairly skillful artists—skillful enough in any case to sell their sketches to the side-show patrons. The major trouble they had was walking. This was because the actions of the right leg were controlled by the right brain, and the left leg by the left brain. Needless to say, these curiosities were much in demand by circus owners, and the boys earned up to a thousand dollars a week.

Probably the fattest man who ever lived was John H. Craig, a native of Kentucky. When he was a year old he weighed 80 pounds. At two, he weighed 206. When he died at the age of thirty-eight, he tipped the scales at nearly half a ton. He earned an excellent living in several circus side shows simply by sitting in an enormous chair and allowing people to gape in awe at his huge bulk. Happily, he left a good-sized estate to his widow—whose weight never exceeded 122.

Eli Bowen and Charles Tripp exhibited themselves in side shows as a team. Eli was the possessor of a handsome and perfectly formed body from the hips up; but he had no legs. Charles's body was equally perfectly proportioned, except that he had no arms. Both were intelligent and well-educated men. Charles Tripp shaved himself, brushed his teeth, smoked cigarettes, wrote in an excellent, flourishing style of penmanship, and painted pictures with his feet. Sometimes, as a part of their act, they rode a tandem bicycle— Bowen sitting in the front saddle doing the steering, and Tripp in the back pumping the pedals. "Watch your step, and don't trip on me," Tripp would say to Bowen. And Bowen would reply, "Okay, but just keep your hands off me." This act always brought down the house.

A man named Billy Wells surely had the hardest head in all known history. His skull was three times as thick as an ordinary human's. In his act, he balanced a six-inch-thick block of granite on top of his head and allowed it to be broken to bits by a sledge hammer. His assistant also splintered a one-and-a-half-inch pine plank over Billy's head. Apparently this kind of daily punishment never bothered him. He was always bright and alert—and he lived to be seventy years old.

During the past few years, the interest in side-show freaks has died out. The big shows do not include them on the bill, and most of the smaller ones have followed suit. Now and again you may see a tent of freaks at carnivals and county fairs. But American show-goers have come to regard freaks as objects of pity rather than of curiosity. For all practical purposes, the side show is as obsolete as the street parade.

Customers flock to the circus as avidly as they did a century ago. But the public's interest today lies in the glorified spectaculars, the color, the drama, the excitement of the big show itself.

The circus retains its original magic. Basically it has never changed. But peoples' taste in entertainment has changed—and to that extent the never-changing, ever-changing circus has changed with it.

Display #11

GARGANTUA THE GREAT

Wᴉᴛʜ the possible exception of Jumbo, the most renowned animal in circus history was an African gorilla named Gargantua. For the eleven years that he was with the Ringlings—from 1938 to 1949—he was the circus's number-one attraction, getting top billing on posters and advertisements over all the biggest-name human stars.

He was also probably the most dangerous animal ever kept in captivity. Gargy, as the circus people called him with a sort of off-beat affection, had a dedicated urge to kill every *homo sapiens* who accidentally ventured near him. On more than one occasion, he actually tried to trick people into coming within the lethal range of his powerful arms. During his years with the circus, no one ever entered his cage when he was in it, and he was never allowed out of it. The circus management lived in constant fear that he might one day escape, perhaps in a railroad wreck or because a keeper grew careless in securing the locks on his cage. Knowing that if he ever got loose among helpless humans he would at once embark upon a rampage of mass murder, and that it would be virtually impossible to recapture him, the circus animal men had strict orders to shoot him on sight if ever any such crisis developed.

Yet the amazing thing is that he started out life in the civilized world of humans as the pampered pet of a gentle little old lady in Brooklyn, New York.

Gargantua was found in the jungles of the Camaroons, a mountainous district of central Africa, when a party of native hunters killed his mother. He was then just a month old, but he was bigger and more active than an ordinary gorilla of his tender age. He was taken to the native encampment and there nursed like a human baby by a woman who had just lost her own baby in childbirth. This should have instilled into him some of the milk of human kindness, but unfortunately it didn't.

At the age of a year, the little gorilla was sold to an animal collector who put him on a ship bound for New York. Because of his exceptional size and good (gorilla-type) looks, the animal man expected to get a good price for him. But sometime during the voyage, and apparently for no reason at all, one of the crew members threw a vial of acid into his face. The ship's captain never discovered who had perpetrated such a cruel and senseless trick, nor why; but the incident left Gargy with deep burn scars on the side of his face which twisted his mouth into a permanent and terrifying snarl. Very likely it was this acid-throwing attack that created in the big brute's little brain what was later on to develop into a lifelong hatred of anything human.

His facial disfigurement having greatly lowered his value as a zoo exhibit, the gorilla's owner sold him at a cut price to a lady in Brooklyn named Mrs. Gertrude Linz, whose hobby was making pets of unusual animals. She gave him the name of Buddy—and the free run of her house.

Mrs. Linz employed a trainer, one Richard Kroener, to teach Buddy good manners and a few simple tricks. She even had a pair of shoes especially made for him so that he could walk upright. For the next five years, Buddy was a reasonably well-behaved household pet, although sometimes difficult. By now he weighed more than four hundred pounds, and his strength was prodigious. This fact was dramatically brought to Mrs. Linz's attention one day when she saw him pick up one of her cats in his great fingers and squeeze it to a pulp. She at once decided that he was no longer the kind of pet that should be allowed to run around loose. The next day she had him put into a cage.

Now in his wild state in the African mountain jungles, the gorilla is a fairly peaceful character—if he is let alone and not molested. He keeps constantly on the move through the rain forests with his family, eating bamboo shoots, wild fruits and vegetables, as well as termites and ants, and sleeping in trees where the males of the family build a new nest almost every night. Gorillas, alone of all animals, can even tie simple knots with vines to keep the nest securely fastened to the tree's limbs.

Ordinarily, in his nomadic wanderings, a gorilla ambles idly along in a lazy, stoop-shouldered manner, touching the ground at every step with his knuckles. But when he is alarmed, he draws himself to his full height (which is very nearly that of a man's), throws back his big cannonball of a head, bares his long fangs, beats on his huge barrel chest with his clenched fists, and lets out a blood-chilling Tarzan-type roar that sends all the other jungle animals scurrying for their lives. This act is largely a bluff, for no other animal of the forest would dare to challenge a full-grown male gorilla. So great is his strength that he could decapitate a lion with one swipe of his tremendous arms. All the other jungle creatures know this, as do the African tribesmen, and so the gorilla lives for the most part in placid peace.

But when he is caged, the average gorilla becomes mean and unpredictable, and his keepers approach him with the utmost care. Buddy, once he was incarcerated, developed this meanness to a dangerously homicidal degree.

On any number of occasions, Richard Kroener was taken

unaware when he thought that Buddy was asleep, grabbed by the arm, jerked to the side of the cage, and savagely mauled and bitten. At this stage of Buddy's life—he was then six years old—Mrs. Linz decided that for the well-being of all concerned she had better get rid of him.

It so happened that at this time John Ringling North was in the market for a gorilla. In fact he had just spent several thousand dollars in an unsuccessful attempt to have a grown one captured in the Congo. He happily bought Buddy for ten thousand dollars.

Obviously a pet name such as Buddy was a great deal too mild and uninspiring for such a ferocious-looking animal. After several days of frantic brain-storming in the circus press department, somebody was hit by a lightning bolt of genius and came up with the perfect name—Gargantua.

In 1938, Roland Butler—who along with Dexter Fellows and Bill Doll was one of the all-time great circus press agents—was beating the publicity drums for the Ringlings. The thought of buying a little old Brooklyn lady's pet was not his idea of how "the world's most terrifying living creature" should have been acquired. Forthwith, he took a crew of roustabouts out into the scrub-pine and cabbage-palm wilderness a few miles from the circus winter quarters in Sarasota, chopped out a large area of subtropical vegetation, uprooted a number of trees, and in general made the place a shambles. He then took pictures of the scene and used it as a background for a gory poster depicting the capture of the great beast. Presumably a clutch of African natives, and probably a white hunter or two, had been killed in the savage encounter.

Not long after Gargantua arrived in Sarasota, John North himself furnished Butler with a hot piece of copy for the press. He was explaining to some visiting reporters how, a day or so before, Gargy had reached out through the bars,

nabbed a passing roustabout by the arm, pulled him against
the side of the cage, nearly choked him to death, and lacer-
ated his shoulder. In his enthusiasm, North backed up too
close to the bars. "The guy," he was saying, "was walking
along about here when—" At that point, Gargantua flashed
out one of his long arms, clutched North by the coat sleeve,
pulled him up against the bars, and began to chew on
his arm. North was rescued, and rushed off to a hospital. The
story made just about every paper in the country—and made
just about every reader impatient to see the terrible animal.

In his prime, Gargantua weighed something better than
650 pounds, stood five feet six inches tall, and had an arm
spread of nine feet. Since all gorillas have a delicate con-
stitution when exposed to weather other than that of the
Camaroon or Congo rain forests, and are especially suscep-
tible to lung disorders, North had a special air-conditioned
cage built for his star attraction. The temperature inside
was a constant 76 degrees, and the humidity a constant 50.
In the beginning, North attempted to furnish the cage with
a few luxurious touches of the civilization that Gargy had
been accustomed to when he lived with Mrs. Linz—a chair,
a couple of benches, a bed, a trapeze, and a swing. But the
moment he saw these fancy trappings, the big ape splintered
them to smithereens. His keeper finally settled for providing
him with a chain trapeze for exercise, and an automobile
tire which was also suspended from a heavy chain. When the
mood struck him, Gargy yanked down the chains with one
tremendous jerk. According to circus press releases, a blanket
was put into his cage each night for him to sleep on.
But each morning, when he woke up, he ripped the blanket
to shreds. A new blanket was needed every day for eleven
years, which added up to better than four thousand blankets.

It should be explained that Gargantua's cage was divided into two compartments so that he could be shifted

from one to the other for the purposes of house cleaning. His keepers discovered that the best way to move him was to carry a live black snake and wave it in front of the bars. All gorillas are deadly afraid of snakes, and Gargantua was no exception. When he saw the snake he quickly retreated into the adjoining room and heavy bars were clanged down behind him. Nobody took any unnecessary chances with Gargy.

However, reporter Robert Lewis Taylor, in his book *Center Ring,* quoted Gargy's trainer as saying that, in his opinion, the big ape would cheerfully wade through a whole swamp of black snakes to get a good, unobstructed crack at him.

In 1941, John North heard of a female gorilla, almost as big as Gargantua, that was for sale. She was owned by a wealthy sportswoman, Mrs. Kenneth Hoyt, who caught her eleven years before when the Hoyts were on a safari in Africa. As Mrs. Linz had done with Gargantua, Mrs. Hoyt took the infant ape into her home as a pet. She named her M'Toto (which means "little girl" in Swahili) and employed a keeper to take care of her. But as the little girl grew up she became too difficult to handle. She had a bad habit of biting Mrs. Hoyt's servants in a playful manner as well as, on occasion, her guests. When she saw that M'Toto was too much for her, Mrs. Hoyt sold her to John North.

North, a master showman as his uncle John had been, thereupon got a blockbuster of an idea. He announced to the American public that he had purchased, at great expense and trouble, a bride for Gargantua; and that the two would be married at the Sarasota winter quarters in the presence of qualified members of the press. From thenceforth, North envisioned, the two would live together in marital bliss, and hopefully raise a large family of simian circus stars.

The circus people had built an air-conditioned cage for

M'Toto identical with that of Gargantua's. When the cages were pushed together, and the bars between them lifted so that the newlyweds could meet for the first time, Gargy's immediate response was to smash M'Toto in the face with a large head of cabbage and bite her on the arm. The bride's reaction to this loving approach was to pelt Gargantua with an assortment of oranges, cabbages, and grapefruit. The pair finally separated of their own accord, the bars were shut down, and each of them lived happily forever after in separate cages.

Both gorillas ate about twenty pounds of food each day. Their diet included raw vegetables, fruit, eggs, milk, fried chicken, and steak. Gargantua ate half a dozen chocolate bars for dessert. With true feminine delicacy, M'Toto topped off her meals by eating the petals of red roses.

Gargantua died of a lung ailment in 1949. M'Toto died in 1968 at the ripe old age of thirty-eight.

Gargy's place was taken in the Ringling menagerie by a handsome young gorilla whose official name is Gargantua II, but who is familiarly known as Tony. He is almost as big as the original Gargantua was, his fur is dark gray, and, of course, his face is unmarked by acid burns. Thus far, Tony has shown no signs of wanting to destroy the human race—although he strides up and down across his cage presenting a mean-looking visage to his viewers, and looking as though he might be secretly harboring some such dank and grim intent. Up to now, it is said that he has made no obvious attempt to lure anyone within range of his huge arms; but his keepers, remembering Gargantua I, are being extremely careful.

In her later years, M'Toto became a television fan, and so did Tony. A color set was placed just outside their cages where they could see it—but not reach it lest they smash in the picture tube and electrocute themselves. Tony still watches TV every day. His favorite programs are musical shows. And he always watches when a performance of the circus is being telecast. His keepers say that he is especially fascinated by the antics of the clowns.

Display #12

"HERE COME THE CLOWNS!"

T ony, the Ringling gorilla, isn't the only individual who likes clowns. The Joey has been an indispensable fixture of the circus since time out of mind. Every clown, regardless of the costume he wears or the act he puts on, is called a Joey. This is in honor of the great Joseph Grimaldi, the first comic character to adorn his face with paint of assorted colors and wear outlandish clothes. Strangely enough, Grimaldi never appeared in a circus, only on the stages of English, French, and Italian music halls. But even so he has become the patron saint of all circus clowns.

The ancestor of the modern clown was the court jester of the Middle Ages, usually called the "king's fool." He wore a multicolored costume liberally bedecked with bells that jingled merrily when he walked and hopped about. His function was to keep the king amused and lighten the burdens of royalty with funny antics and jokes. Since he was not considered to be very bright he could get away with wisecracks that would have led anyone else in the royal court directly to the executioner's block. Many jesters, however, were extremely intelligent men. In the guise of kidding the king they were often able indirectly to give him wise counsel and advice.

The Pierrot of the early French theater was the first clown to wear white-face make-up and dress in the traditional peaked red cap and loose white ruffled suit that is still generally referred to as a "clown suit." Pierrot was the transition from the jester to today's Joey.

In the pioneer days of the American circus, when there was only one ring and thus only one act going on at a time, most clowns sang, cracked jokes, and did comic monologues. Dan Rice was the most famous example of this clown genre. But the talking clown went out with the expansion of the circus to the great three-ring spectacle that it has become. Now the Joeys perform their gags strictly in pantomime.

The chief role of the clown in the circus of today is to keep everybody amused between the big spectacular acts so that there is never a dull moment between the first walk-around and the final blast of the ringmaster's whistle. His life is not an easy one. He gets clobbered over the head with slap-sticks, stumbles over the ring equipment as well as his own feet, and in general suffers a considerable physical beating. It goes without saying that most of the good clowns are trained athletes.

The acrobatic clowns—the tumblers, wire walkers, and bareback riders—are often far more skilled then the be-spangled stars. A riding clown, for example, must know how to tumble off a running horse without injuring himself, and at the same time make it appear to look like a clumsy accident that sends the audience off into gales of guffaws.

The same goes for the wire-walking clown. When he pretends to make a slip, loses his balance, and then manages to catch himself at the last instant, he must do it with split-second timing lest he actually fall off the wire and break his neck. To make it even more hazardous, he performs in a baggy, cumbersome costume instead of the regular acrobat's close-fitting tights.

In clown lingo, all acts are called gags. And some gags are ageless. One gag that has been a sure-fire hit for

a hundred and fifty years was described by Samuel Clemens
in his immortal *Huckleberry Finn*.

This is how Clemens told it through Huck's young and
innocent eyes:

"It was a powerful fine sight to see the horses running
around the ring faster and faster, and the riders standing up
on them dancing, first with one foot in the air and then the
other. Everybody clapped their hands and went just about
wild.

"Then by and by a drunken man tried to get into the ring;
said he wanted to ride; said he could ride as well as anybody that ever was. The ringmaster argued and tried to keep
him out, but he wouldn't listen, and the whole show come to
a standstill. Then the people begun to hollar at him, and
yell 'Throw him out!' So the ringmaster, he made a little
speech, and said he hoped there wouldn't be no disturbance,
and if the man would promise he wouldn't make no more
trouble he would let him ride if he thought he could stay
on the horse. So everybody laughed and said all right, and
the man got on.

"The minute he was on, the horse begun to rip and tear
and jump and cavort around, with two circus men hanging
on to his bridle trying to hold him, and the drunken man
hanging onto his neck, and his heels flying into the air every
jump, and the whole crowd of people standing up and laughing till tears rolled down their faces. And at last, sure enough,
for all the circus men could do, the horse broke loose and
away he went round and round the ring, with that drunk
laying down on him and hanging to his neck, with first one leg
hanging most to the ground on one side, and the t'other
one on t'other side, and the people just goin' crazy.

"It warn't funny to me, though. I was all of a tremble
to see his danger. But pretty soon he struggled up astraddle
and grabbed the bridle, a-reeling this way and that; and the
next minute he sprung up and dropped the bridle and *stood!*
And the horse was going like a house afire too. He just
stood up there a-sailing around as easy and comfortable as

if he warn't ever drunk in his life. And then he begun to
pull off his clothes and sling them into the air. And there
he was, slim and handsome, and dressed the gaudiest and
prettiest you ever saw. And everybody just howled with pleasure
and astonishment.

"Then the ringmaster, he seen how he had been fooled,
and he was just about the *sickest* ringmaster you ever did see,
I reckon."

With only slight variations, almost the identical act has
been "wowing" circus audiences ever since.

Every individual clown creates his own make-up, his
costumes, and, for the most part, his gags. Even in a circus
empire as big as the current Ringling's, which carries something like a hundred clowns with each unit, no two of them
look exactly alike. Each clown's make-up is his trade-mark,
his exclusive property. Often he may experiment for years to
achieve precisely the effect he wants. And from then on that
character is his alone. In the world of the circus there is an
unwritten law that no other clown may ever copy it.

It is almost impossible to put clowns into definite cate-
gories. Many circus people, however, agree that there are
four basic types—the Auguste, the Grotesque, the Character,
and the Midget. Obviously there are many varieties of each,
much too numerous to try to classify.

Generally, the Auguste paints his face with a combination
of contrasting colors, puts on a big red putty nose, wears
out-sized shoes, and affects a costume so ridiculous that it
defies description. Often his baggy pants are striped or
polka-dotted. An Auguste's specialty is getting in everybody
else's way and in general making a nuisance of himself.
While the roustabouts are taking down the rigging of the
act that has just finished and setting up for the act that is to
follow, the Auguste tries to lend a hand, gives advice, helps
move the props, trips over guy wires and falls flat on his

face, and ends up by seemingly throwing everything into utter confusion.

The Grotesque wears the most outrageous getup he can think of. Usually his face is painted white, with a red nose and a great red smear of a mouth that literally stretches from ear to ear. Sometimes he pads his stomach and hips to make himself appear grossly fat, his pantaloons are trimmed with fancy fringe.

The late Felix Adler, known for years as the King of Clowns, was a typical Grotesque. He carried a tiny parasol, wore a tiny hat with a long-stemmed flower growing out of its top, and led a trained pig on a leash. When the pig awkwardly climbed up and over a small stepladder, much to Adler's apparent amazement, it always brought down the house. Like most clowns, Adler became a circus fan as a small boy, ran away from his home in Clinton, Iowa, at the age of twelve, got his first job under the big top carrying water and feed for the elephants and horses, and finally graduated into clowning.

The Character clown is best exemplified by Emmett Kelly, the famous tramp. Kelly started out as a cartoonist on a Midwest newspaper, and in the process created a tramp character that he soon began to identify with himself. It wasn't long before he deserted the drawing board and became a circus clown.

Kelly dresses in a tattered and much-patched suit that is many sizes too big for him. His hat looks as if it has been run over by a truck, and his huge shoes, with his toes sticking out of them, seem to have long since fallen apart. In his act he quickly identifies with his audience and gets their amused sympathy by his total inability ever to do anything right. He tries valiantly to make a go of everything he attempts, but like most people in real life he never quite succeeds.

He comes out with a large broom and starts to sweep the dirt out of the arena; but he soon gives up the job as hopeless and just leans wistfully on his broom, staring up at the crowd in pure frustration. He begins to juggle rubber balls, but keeps dropping them. He runs around under the trapeze artists with his arms outstretched to catch them if they fall; but they never do. He tries to sweep up a splash of light made by an overhead spotlight, but just as soon as the job is almost done the light moves to another place. As he continues his fruitless career of failure, his woebegone facial expression—accented by a large, white, down-turned mouth set in a dark stubble of unshaven whiskers—is the saddest in the world.

Another typical example of the Character is the clown who has his trousers rigged with wire so that they fly up above his knees every time he tips his hat to someone in the stands.

The Midget clowns are in a class by themselves. They dress up as dogs or elephants or elves, or as babies licking on out-size lollipops while being wheeled along in carriages by normal-sized clowns dressed as their mothers. Otherwise they usually adopt variations of the Auguste or Grotesque costumes. You will never see a Midget moving slowly. He is usually scampering along as rapidly as his short little legs will take him.

It has been mentioned that circus folks think it is good luck to touch a clown, and that it is especially good luck to touch a Midget. The little fellows like to be touched, for they believe it brings *them* good luck too. So if you happen to walk by a Midget clown the next time you're at a circus, don't hesitate to reach out and touch him. He'll be delighted.

Clown gags are constantly changing and new ones are always being added. But, like Huck Finn's drunken bareback rider, there are a few standard classics that get roars of laughter and applause year after year.

One is the clown fire department. A group of clown carpenters hastily rig up a flimsy house in the arena and a clown couple, usually dressed as a newlywed bride and groom, move in. Suddenly the house catches on fire and smoke and flames pour out the windows. With a raucous screeching of sirens and clanging of bells, an absurd-looking fire truck rushes to the scene. The clown firemen rescue the bride and groom, but they can't put out the fire. Their hoses get tangled up, and when they are finally straightened, only a drop or two of water trickles out. Then another clown runs up with a small glass of water, throws it on the fire, and instantly extinguishes it. This is one of the oldest clown gags in the business, and you will rarely go to the circus without seeing some sort of variation of it.

Another gag that never fails is the small-car trick. A small foreign-type car drives once around the arena then stops and the driver gets out. Then as many as twenty Midget clowns pile out of the car after him. Sometimes the last one leads a small donkey. How so many people, even Midgets, can get themselves into such a tiny automobile is a well-kept trade secret.

Every circus has its clown policemen. A typical cop-clown gag goes about like this.

Two clowns start an argument. A cop clown, usually a Midget, runs up and attempts to arrest them. The two fighters turn on the cop and begin to beat him up with clubs. At this, other cops rush in to help, and this starts a free-for-all in which everybody is slugging everyone else. In the end, the clowns who started the fight in the first place run out of the ring with all the cops chasing them. During this interlude the circus roustabouts have had time to set up the rigging for the next acrobatic or animal act.

As a rule, the clowns open every show with what they call a "walk-around," in which all of them parade around the arena—waving at the crowd, sometimes stepping into the lower rows of seats to shake hands and say hello to children, tripping over each other, stopping now and then to do their particular specialties, and in general indulging in mass tom-foolery. Their appearance is always greeted with howls of laughter and whoops—especially from every kid in the place —of: "Here come the clowns!" The "walk-around" always gets the crowd into the proper mood for the big show that is to follow.

All the clowns in the circus share a common dressing room. This is known as Clown Alley, and most of the time it is a modified madhouse. Clowns are by nature a fun-loving lot, and usually act as crazily off stage as on. I visited Clown Alley once or twice when I was writing a story about them—and it was a laugh a minute. The long rows of dressing tables were littered with wigs, putty noses, tubes of grease paint and cold cream, costumes, props, and all the endless paraphernalia of clowndom. I quickly learned that the Joeys' greatest delight, when not acting before the audience, is playing tricks on one another.

They rig up a fellow clown's chair so that when he sits down in it, it will collapse. They mix up grease paints to the utter confusion of the man who is trying to make up. They hide costumes so that the fellow who is trying to make a quick change can't find the article he needs. Every clown is at heart a zany. And the word zany itself, as a matter of fact, came from an old medieval name for a clown. In those ancient days, clowns were also called Jack Puddings and Merry Andrews.

The urge to be a clown hits almost everybody at one time or another—even if it is only the fellow at the party who cavorts around with a lampshade on his head. Many sedate businessmen, who fifty weeks out of the year may be dignified bank presidents, or sales executives, or lawyers, spend their vacations traveling with the circus as clowns. They do it, of course, without pay, simply because it is more fun than any other kind of vacation they can think of.

One of America's best-known motion picture stars—who became circus struck when he once played the part of a clown in a film—occasionally works a week or two as a "walk-around" clown. Naturally his name never appears on the program, nor does anyone recognize him under his make-up.

I did it just once. One afternoon Count Nicholas, who was then the Ringling ringmaster and is now an executive with the Hetzer Circus, gave me permission to dress up as a clown and take part in the "walk-around." The boys in Clown Alley had a field day when they made up my face and put me into a hastily got-up costume. I was probably the worst clown who ever walked around. But then I imagine that most amateurs who play at being clowns feel the same way about it.

Not long ago the Ringling Brothers and Barnum & Bailey management established a school for clowns at Venice, Florida, the new winter quarters, which is just a few miles from Sarasota. The head instructor is Mel Miller, who was a star Ringling clown for many years. Here young men who want to learn to be professional clowns get expert training in all the tricks of the trade. The students who show the most promising aptitude for clowning graduate to regular circus jobs.

The circus, which will certainly always be with us, will never be without clowns any more than it will be without elephants, wild animals, and acrobats.

Display #13

THE DARING YOUNG MEN—AND WOMEN

THE clowns have finished their between-acts foolishness and have scampered out of the arena. Now a battery of spotlights blaze and a group of performers, garbed in spangled tights and covered by silken cloaks, slide gracefully into center ring and take a bow. The crowd's laughter cuts off instantly and is replaced by an expectant silence. For these are the aerialists, the flyers, the daring young men and women on the flying trapeze.

High over their heads, almost a hundred feet above the sawdust covered floor, are two tiny platforms. These, too, are about a hundred feet apart. Under them is stretched a springy woven-rope net. As the ringmaster steps up to the microphone to announce their act, they drop their cloaks to the ground and climb swiftly and effortlessly hand-over-hand up ropes (or "webs" as circus people call them) to the platforms. On one stand two slender, athletically trim men and a girl. Opposite them, on the other platform, is a single man who is bigger and heavier. The trio are the flyers. The single man is the catcher.

From both platforms the aerialists unhook a trapeze and swing it back and forth until they establish a rhythm. Then one of the flyers hurls himself out on the trapeze, experimentally, and lands back on his platform. Meanwhile the catcher has been doing the same thing. Now the catcher pulls himself up onto the trapeze, securely hooks his knees over it, and hangs head downward, his arms outstretched, all the while swinging back and forth.

One of the young flyers on the opposite platform grasps his own trapeze, holds it for a moment while he rubs his hands dry, and then sails out. Midway between the two platforms he releases his hold on the trapeze, flies through the air, perhaps turns a somersault as he does so, and is caught in the strong arms of the catcher. The audience yells its approval.

Then, one after the other, the remaining flyers, the man and the girl, repeat the performance. Each time they do so, their acts get trickier, more dangerous and more exciting. After single somersaults, they do double ones and then triples. This is perhaps the most thrilling spectacle anyone has ever seen under the big top.

It is also one of the most hazardous. For like all acrobatic acts, it is much more risky than the kinkers make it seem. Now and then one of the flyers misses his hand-hold on the catcher and falls into the protective net. This kind of miss is rarely, if ever, faked—especially in the complicated doubles and triples. For unless an aerialist falls into the net intentionally—as all of them do when the act is over—he can break his neck as surely as if he had landed on the hard ground.

Just as a student rider first learns how to fall off a horse without hurting himself, so does a novice aerialist learn how to fall into the net. If he lands headfirst, it may well result in a broken neck. A feet-first landing can very likely break an ankle or a leg. A flyer must land on his back, ready to bounce upright instantly, to avoid injury. If he falls accidentally and sees that he won't be able to land on his back he rolls his body into a ball, ducks his head between his hands and knees, and hopes for the best.

The first flyer was a young Frenchman named Jules

Leotard, who, in addition to originating the aerial act, gave his name to the tight-fitting costume that all acrobats—as well as ballet dancers—wear. In the mid-1800s, his thrilling new performance became the sensation of Paris and London.

In the beginning, Leotard simply swung from one flying trapeze to another. Then he got the brilliant idea of adding a second performer to his act, the catcher, who would swing from the opposite trapeze and grab him in mid-air as he flew. Thus he created an entirely new form of circus acrobatics.

Aerial flying has become tremendously more complicated and thrilling since Leotard's time. Today there are dozens of flying teams in circuses large and small. But the daring aerialists have never made this sensational act any less dangerous for themselves, nor less breath-stopping for the audiences who gasp in wonder as the performers fly through the air.

Next to the aerial flyers for thrills, and sometimes even more so, are the high-wire walkers. Along with tumbling, walking on a rope or wire was the first of the acrobatic acts developed in the circuses of medieval times.

The greatest wire-walking team ever seen was the Wallenda family, who joined the Big One in the late 1920s. Working forty feet or more up, without a safety net, as many as seven Wallendas were on the wire at the same time. Four men walked on the wire balancing a long pole across their shoulders. Two others stood on the pole, and they too had a pole on their shoulders. At the top of the pyramid a girl stood balanced on a chair. Sometimes they did this death-defying act riding bicycles across the wire instead of walking. In the case of the intrepid Wallendas, the word "death-defying" was not just a Barnum-type adjective. On several occasions they have fallen, and two or three of them have been killed. But younger members of the family, as they grow up, step on the wire to take the places of their elders. Occasionally other wire walkers have joined the act and assumed the Wallenda name. And the fabulous Wallendas go on.

Another fantastic funambulist was an Argentinian named Con Colleano. Dressed as a bullfighter, he did a bolero dance on the high wire. To cap his act, he did a backward somersault, pulled off his tight-fitting toreador pants in mid-air, and landed again on the wire as lightly and surely as a robin glides down and perches on the branch of a tree.

Without any question, the most dazzling and daredevilish rope-walking stunt of all time was performed in the summer of 1859 by a famous French funambulist by the name of Jean François Gravelet, who billed himself as Blondin. He had been performing in Niblo's Garden in New York City when he was struck by the brainstorm of walking across Niagara Falls on a tightrope. The news of his forthcoming feat was ballyhooed by P. T. Barnum and made front page stories in all the newspapers. Barnum himself was not the sponsor of the spectacle, but he cashed in on it by chartering special trains from New York to Niagara.

Blondin and his assistants worked nearly a month to prepare for the big event. First a light line was taken from the American to the Canadian side of the river. There are conflicting stories about this. Some say that it was carried across by boat, which would have been the easiest and simplest way—others that a prize was offered to the first boy who could land a kite on the opposite shore. The latter seems more in keeping with Barnum's publicity style. In any case, the light cord was used to haul a big rope from one bank of the river to the other. The rope on which Blondin did his walking was more than three inches thick. It was secured by heavy guy-ropes which

16. Lillemor Mollor and her Lipizzaner stallion taking a bow. *(Ringling Brothers and Barnum & Bailey)*

17. A typical steam calliope. No old-time circus was complete without one. *(New York Public Library)*

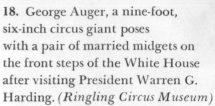

18. George Auger, a nine-foot, six-inch circus giant poses with a pair of married midgets on the front steps of the White House after visiting President Warren G. Harding. (*Ringling Circus Museum*)

19. The idea of dieting would have horrified Alice from Dallas. Her fat was her fortune. (*Ringling Circus Museum*)

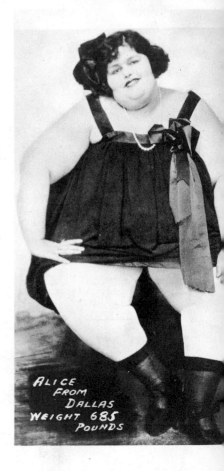

ALICE FROM DALLAS WEIGHT 685 POUNDS

20. Lionel, Barnum & Bailey's "dog-faced boy." An avid student, he could speak and write seven languages. (*Museum of the City of New York*)

21. Gargantua and his intended bride, M'Toto. This must be a composite picture — they were never friendly enough to pose together. (*Ringling Circus Museum*)

22. Lou Jacobs —
called the King of the Clowns.
(Ringling Brothers and Barnum & Bailey)

23. The famous clown, Felix Adler,
with his trained pig.
(Ringling Circus Museum)

24. The daring young men — and girl — on the flying trapeze. These are the Flying Waynes. (*Ringling Brothers and Barnum & Bailey*)

25. The Wallendas and their famous "pyramid" tight-wire act. Members of the original family are still performing today. (*Museum of the City of New York*)

26. The Marinkas perform one of the world's most difficult balancing tricks. (*Ringling Brothers and Barnum & Bailey*)

27. The famous Clyde Beatty and his "pets." He now has his own show: Clyde Beatty-Cole Brothers, which travels under canvas. *(Ringling Circus Museum)*

28. Adela Smieja, "The Lady of the Cats," rewards one of them for a trick well done. *(Ringling Brothers and Barnum & Bailey)*

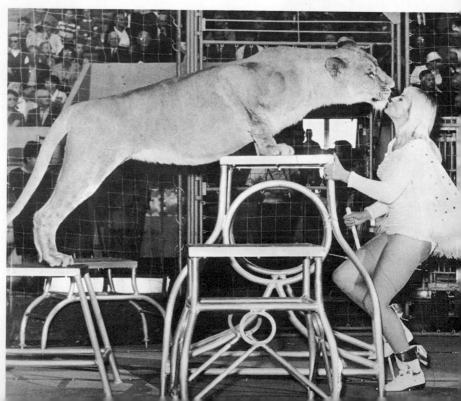

29. Trained bears have been circus favorites since the traveling circuses of the Middle Ages.
(*Ringling Brothers and Barnum & Bailey*)

30. Everybody wants to get into the act including the equestrian chimps.
(*Ringling Brothers and Barnum & Bailey*)

31. A Siberian tiger rides an Appaloosa horse. The trainer is Adolph Althoff. The horse actually trembles with fear, but he goes through the act like a trouper. (*Ringling Brothers and Barnum & Bailey*)

were fastened to trees and rocks on the river's edges. The main rope was 1300 feet long and was suspended several hundred feet above the roaring waters of the falls. A reporter for the New York *Tribune* estimated that no less than 12,000 spectators assembled to see the show. On the American side, people had to pay admission to get into an amusement park for a good view. There was no charge for those who watched from Canada.

On the afternoon of July 1, the great show began. Blondin stepped out on the rope as nonchalantly as if he was taking a Sunday stroll in the park. Every few yards he stopped to dance a jig, balance on one foot, lie down on the rope, hang from it by his hands, fling himself upright again and run along for a few steps. High over the middle of the river he lowered a string to the *Maid of the Mist,* a small boat that carried sight-seers through the billows of spume and spray below the falls—just as a similar boat of the same name still does today. The boat's captain tied a bottle of wine to the string. Blondin pulled it up, drank the wine, and then went on to Canada. After a few minutes' rest, he walked back—this time with fewer didoes and of course in much less time.

During the next few days, the fearless Frenchman made several more crossings. Once he did it blindfolded, once with wooden buckets on his feet, once pushing a wheelbarrow ahead of him. Another time he carried a chair and a small charcoal stove. Halfway across, he calmly sat down on the chair, cooked an egg on the stove, and ate it before going on.

On his final trip, Blondin offered to carry anyone in the crowd at the amusement park on his back. As might have been expected, he had no takers. Thereupon he pressed his terrified manager into service as his unwilling passenger. Blondin was a small man, and his manager was heavier than he was. Carrying a long balancing pole in his hands, and with the fear-stricken manager clinging to him in a death grip, he started across the rope. The weight must have been a little more than he had counted on, for Blondin had to stop a number of time during the crossing for long rests. But at last he arrived on the Canadian side safe and sound. Perhaps the happiest man in either the United States or Canada at that particular moment was the shaking and nerve-shattered manager as he hopped down once more onto solid ground.

But Blondin's nerves, if he had any at all, must have been steel wires. He rested awhile to regain his strength and get back his wind. And then he made the return trip—*on stilts!*

Later, in his native Paris, Blondin walked on a rope across the Seine—not nearly so thrilling one would imagine as walking over Niagara—and between the lofty towers of Notre Dame.

Blondin continued to electrify audiences in both Europe and America with his rope-walking stunts until he was seventy-two years old—an age at which most ordinary men find it tiring to walk more than a few blocks down a city sidewalk.

If there is any possible way of adding a new twist to an act, circus acrobats will find it. Pole-balancing is a typical example. A man balances a tall pole on his head. A young girl shinnies up to a perch on the top of the pole. There she begins to juggle hoops or balls. As if that has seemed too easy up to now, the man climbs onto the seat of a unicycle, the pole with the juggling girl still balanced on his forehead, and pedals around the ring.

A German acrobat billed as Desperado thrilled customers at the original Barnum and Bailey Circus with what was

known as the Terrrible Leap for Life. From a platform
that was eighty feet high, he did a swan dive onto a
sloping slide on the ground which was covered with a
thin layer of corn meal as lubrication. The slide curved
down and then upward again, and Desperado landed on
his chest and stomach, swooped down, up and out through
the air into a net that was twenty feet away.

Another famous high dive is done from the very top
of the arena, probably one hundred feet above the sawdust
floor. A spotlight picks up the stunt man as he stands
tiptoe on his tiny platform. The drums in the band begin
a long roll as he stands with arms outstretched before
him. As the drum rolls reach a crescendo he dives—straight
down. A rope fastened to his ankle jerks him to an abrupt
stop when his head is no more than eight inches from the
ground. A loose knot, the slightest stretching of the rope,
any smallest miscalculation, would put a sudden and permanent end to the act for all time.

Looping the loop on a bicycle was a dangerous, yet
fairly commonplace stunt in the circuses of the early 1900s.
The rider pedaled furiously down a steep incline, shot off
into empty air, looped the loop just as an airplane pilot does,
and landed—if his luck held—on another runway fifty feet
away that led to the ground. Later on the trick was done
with a motorcycle or small automobile. As you may well
imagine, the accident and casualty statistics for loop the
loop artists were astronomic. But the acrobats will try almost anything it if gets a big hand and cheer from the
crowd and builds up their own reputations and salaries.

One all-time popular act is the one in which a man
or a girl or sometimes two people at once are shot out
of a cannon.

The cannon is a huge contraption, bigger than the heaviest piece of actual heavy artillery. When it is wheeled

cumbersomely into place, the performer climbs up a ladder, waves a last good-by to everybody, and lets himself down into the cannon's mouth. After a few moments of breathless waiting, an assistant lights the fuse. With an ear-splitting *boom!* the acrobat is shot out of the big gun accompanied by a huge cloud of smoke. He sails through the air, as much as seventy-five feet high, and then clear across the length of the arena to land in a net. The actual propellant is a spring worked by compressed air. The smoke and boom are for dramatic effect. But like all circus tricks, this is an extremely dangerous one. The most famous "human cannon ball" was a man named Hugo Zacchini, who made this act a feature attraction of the Big One for many years.

No circus act is quite so graceful or pleasing to the eye as the girl who performs on webs and Roman rings. She ascends the dangling webs, not hand over hand, but in a series of slow, graceful body roll-overs that are apparently done without effort, and with all the flawless style and beauty of a ballet dance. Reaching the rings that hang side by side from the top of the arena, she goes through a series of thrilling handstands, loops, and twirls.

Then comes the climax of the act. Inserting her hand and wrist securely into a loop in the web that is attached to a swivel, she begins a series of revolutions that are called plange turns—throwing her body over and over her shoulders to keep going in a continuing circle. As she rolls over at an ever increasing speed, the ringmaster at the microphone begins to count the turns. And it is traditional that the audience take up the count with him, shouting out the numbers in a cadenced chant: ". . . ten . . . eleven . . . twelve . . . fifty-nine . . . seventy-three . . ." —usually up to at least one hundred before she comes to a leisurely stop and is lowered to the ground to take her bows.

For sheer physical stamina, the plange is one of the most exacting of all aerial acts.

Virtually all circus people agree that the greatest aerial artist who ever performed was a small German girl named Lillian Leitzel. For many years, until her tragic death on the rings in 1931, she was the brightest star in the Ringling heavens.

Leitzel was just a tiny thing, less than five feet tall and weighing not quite 100 pounds. She had a slender, beautiful body—her feet were so small that she wore child-size shoes—but her shoulders and upper arms were as well-muscled as those of a bantam-weight boxer. Because of this remarkable shoulder development, she could move on the web and the rings with an ease so effortless that she seemed to float in the air. She did the plange so easily that it seemed more like the flight of a hummingbird than the grueling physical punishment which it was. Each time she hurled her body in a full circle over herself, her shoulder joints were momentarily dislocated, and then instantly snapped back into place by the tremendous muscles. She regularly did more than 100 plange turns at each performance, and her record was 249. Leitzel did the plange equally well with her left arm as with her right.

During her long stay with the Ringling show, she married Alfredo Codona, who is regarded by old-time circus fans as the finest flyer who ever worked on the high trapeze. His style was as graceful as Leitzel's—and, as she did, he made everything look ridiculously easy. So high was their standing as circus luminaries that they were the only performers who were accorded the unheard of privilege of traveling in their own private railroad car.

In February of 1931, while Ringling Brothers and Barnum

& Bailey were in winter quarters at Sarasota, Codona and Leitzel were playing in Europe—he at the Winter Garden in Berlin and she at the Valencia Music Hall in Copenhagen.

On Friday, which happened to be the thirteenth, Lillian was doing a handstand on the Roman rings only twenty feet above the stage when one of the rings snapped. Caught suddenly off balance, she lost her grip on the other ring and fell. In such a short fall, she was unable to twist her body over and land on her feet. Instead she hit the stage squarely with her head. Seemingly only dazed for a moment, she stood up and took her bows to wild applause and cheers from the audience. But once in the wings, she collapsed and was rushed to a hospital. Codona hurried to her from Berlin—but two days later she was dead.

The Leitzel-Codona tragedy was not ended. Alfredo began to take outrageous risks in his act, as though he wanted deliberately to kill himself. Inevitably he had an accident. Instead of killing him, it injured his shoulder so badly that he could never fly on the trapeze again. Meanwhile he had remarried, this time to a circus equestrienne named Vera Bruce. Since he was no longer able to perform, he became Vera's assistant. But having once been such a shining star, he couldn't take his descent from glory. He quit the circus altogether, took a series of menial jobs, and wound up pumping gas at a filling station. He was so embittered and impossible to live with, Vera sued him for divorce.

In her lawyer's office at a meeting to discuss settlement terms, Codona requested a private talk with his wife. The moment the attorney had closed the door, six shots blasted from a heavy pistol. Alfredo had pumped five bullets into Vera's body, and the sixth into his own brain. Both lay dead when the lawyer re-entered the room.

The paths of glory . . .

The grand finale of the aerial acts in the Big One is usually an entire chorus of twenty-five or thirty girls performing a mass ballet dance on the webs. Most of them are beginners at their trade. But every one of them has wonderful dreams of someday becoming as great as the fabulous Lillian Leitzel. Naturally, they don't want to fall and kill themselves as she did. But to reach out and touch the stars they are willing to take their chances.

Display #14

THE ANIMAL FARE

FROM the very beginnings of the circus, people have always been excited and fascinated by the spectacle of wild animals, especially the big cats, being put through their paces by a trainer who is usually armed with nothing more lethal than a whip or a light chair. There is no question in any onlooker's mind that the snarling, clawing lions, leopards, and tigers could turn on the man in a flash and tear him apart. This has happened many times, even to the most careful and skillful trainers. The miracle is that the trainer can handle the great beasts at all and make them do tricks that are completely foreign to their jungle-born natures.

An animal trainer must have great courage, and a sublime confidence in his own power to keep his dangerous charges under complete control at all times. He must also have an instinctive knowledge of what motivates them, both as individuals and in a group. Above all, it is absolutely essential that he possess a natural-born empathy with them, an indefinable something that is usually referred to as a "way with animals."

While a trainer must not fear his animals, he must always respect them. On the other hand, the animals must fear, as well as respect, the trainer. He must be alert and on his toes every second that he is in the cage—for even big cats that have been considered trustworthy for years have suddenly turned on their trainers without warning and chewed or mauled them. Above all, a trainer must be completely without any trace of fear. For any animal, even a dog or a horse, can sense fear in a human and be quick to take advantage of it.

Even so, modern trainers teach and control their beasts with kindness rather than with brutality. They know that if they are needlessly cruel to an animal, that animal will very likely be waiting quietly at all times for a chance to get revenge. A trainer speaks softly to his cats, rewards them after a trick with a small morsel of meat, and constantly visits them in their cages.

Virtually every circus, even the smallest one, has its animal trainer, but there have been a few super-stars that achieved sawdust immortality.

In the France of the Bourbon kings, there was a young man named Jean François Pezon who seemed to have some sort of special affinity with wolves. In those days, wolves were common in Europe and were a great menace to farmers' sheep and cattle. Young Pezon, so the story goes, used to go out into the dense forests, catch a wolf, and lead it back into town by a rope. In time, he collected a dozen or more and taught them to do tricks, like dogs. As the years passed, he added lions and tigers to his act until he finally had the biggest performing menagerie in France. At his death, he passed on his animals and his acts to his sons, and the Pezons continued to be animal trainers for several generations. The last of the Pezon line, whose name also was Jean François, was killed in the cage by a performing lion only a few years ago.

The earliest American animal trainer of note was Isaac Van Amburgh, who was born in Dutchess County, New York, in 1811, and had never had anything to do with animals except perhaps to teach his dog how to sit up and beg. But he seemed to possess that elusive "way with animals." Van Amburgh first came to the public's attention when, at the age of twenty-two, he stepped into a cage of lions and tigers on the stage of a New York City theater and apparently cowed the beasts with intuitive ease. His act became the talk of the city, and in a few years he took to the road with his own show, traveling all over the Eastern coast of the United States and Europe.

Van Amburgh's special forte was the bringing of Bible stories to life in the animal cage. In one of his famous acts, he portrayed Daniel in the lions' den. In another, he trained a lion to lie down with a lamb—and it is said that he later introduced a small boy into the cage to complete the biblical prediction that "a little child shall lead them." History does not record the names of the money-hungry parents who allowed their child to take part in so perilous and senseless a stunt.

Although Van Amburgh died in 1865—not, incidentally, as a result of an accident in the cage—his name continued to be used by a series of circuses until it was absorbed by the owners of the American Circus Corporation in 1908.

The first of the great modern trainers was Carl Hagenbeck, who has been mentioned earlier. He set the pattern for such well-known animal men as Alfred Court, Clyde Beatty, and a girl named Mable Stark.

Alfred Court is considered by a great many circus people to have been the finest animal trainer who ever worked. His methods were kindness, friendliness, and immediate rewards for an act well done. But he was just as quick to punish. He always carried a small whip which he could use with pin-point accuracy. When a lion or a tiger made a mistake, Court's whip flicked painfully against the most sensitive part of the beast's anatomy—but only as a reminder that the animal had done wrong and had to be reminded of it at that very instant so that he would know exactly what the punishment was for and would never make the same error again. Alfred Court ran his act so smoothly that Henry Ringling North, now a vice-president of the Big One, once described it as "seeming as easy and polite as an Arthur Murray class in ballroom dancing."

Clyde Beatty, probably the best known of modern animal trainers, used quite another method. Beatty, in addition to being a superb animal trainer, was also a superb ham. An extremely handsome and personable young man, who later starred in a number of jungle movies, he took a highly theatrical approach. He wore the apparel of a Hollywood-type African white hunter—flaring white riding breeches, shiny riding boots, a belted safari jacket, and a pith helmet. He cracked his long whip so that it sounded like rifle shots, fired blanks from a pistol that he carried in a holster on his hip, and often used a light cane chair to poke into the snarling faces of his animals.

All of this, however, was just for show purposes. He trained his big cats just as every other successful trainer did—with kindness, affection, and rewards for good behavior. Perhaps this made it a little more difficult for him to make them behave well amidst all the sound and fury that went on in the cage.

After spending several seasons with the Ringlings and other shows, interspersed with motion picture roles, he took out a wild animal circus under his own name. Today it has expanded into the Clyde Beatty-Cole Brothers Show, and is one of the few circuses that still play under canvas.

Frank Buck, the famous "Bring 'Em Back Alive" animal collector, played a few seasons with the Ringlings, but never as a trainer inside a cage. He usually only took part in the Grand Entry.

Women animal trainers have always been a rarity. There

have been a few good ones, but only one who has taken on the mantle of greatness. Mable Stark was a young girl from Kentucky, a graduate nurse who had always had a yen to get into a cage and work with the big animals since she saw her first circus in a Kentucky hill town at the age of about eight. She pestered the manager of the Al G. Barnes Circus, a middle-sized traveling show, until at last, to get rid of her, he took her on as an assistant to the star of the animal act.

From the first moment she entered a cageful of lions, Mable demonstrated that she possessed that heaven-given mysterious something that gave her a control over animals. Within a year, she was a circus star in her own right.

She always went into the cage entirely unarmed— no pistol, no chair, not even the slightest whip. She directed her big cats by speaking softly to them, and signaling with her hands and arms. In one magnificent act she had sixteen Bengal tigers in the cage at the same time, probably the greatest number ever handled by a trainer. She wrestled with the huge Bengals, taught them to ride on horses, and ordinarily capped the climax of her hair-raising performance by putting her head in a tiger's mouth.

Mable paid dearly for her daring. She was probably bitten, chewed, clawed, and mauled more times than any other trainer has ever been. But as soon as she was well enough to be on her feet again—as soon as the doctors had mended her broken bones and sewed up her mangled shoulders, back, arms, and face—she went right back into the cage with her cats.

Her worst accident came when two tigers, named Sheik and Zoo, both of which had proved themselves to be potential killers, and both of which had tried to attack her before, jumped her one afternoon when she happened to slip and fall. Sheik almost took one of her legs off, and

Zoo hurried to enjoy a share of the tasty meal. Other animal men rushed to her aid, fought the tigers off and managed to pull her out of the cage. The Ringling management recommended that both Sheik and Zoo be destroyed, but Mable would not allow it. The next season, horribly scarred but unafraid, she was back in the cage with the killers.

Nobody has ever been able to figure out the particular chemistry that puts an animal trainer together.

As was the case when Blondin walked a tightrope across Niagara Falls, perhaps the most hair-raising encounter between a man and a big cat occurred far from a circus ring. Instead it took place in the African bush country, when Carl Akeley, a big-game hunter and animal collector, became the first and only man in known history to kill a leopard with his bare hands.

Akeley had been out on a scouting expedition looking for specimens and was walking back to camp alone in the gathering darkness. Suddenly from the bushes ahead of him he heard a snarling growl, and saw the lithe silhouette of a big female leopard slinking through the shadows only a few yards away. Ake quickly raised his rifle to fire, but as he did so the leopard sailed through the air, her claws extended and her long white fangs bared, and hit him sideways. The force of the impact knocked the gun from his hands, and the leopard sank her teeth into the muscles of his upper right arm.

With his free hand, Ake grabbed her by the throat and began to squeeze. The big cat gagged and loosened her grip. But as Akeley tried slowly and painfully to work his arm out of her mouth, she managed to get another tooth-hold farther down. Again Ake tightened his throat grip, and again she loosened her jaws slightly and he was able to work his mangled arm a little bit more out of her mouth.

As his weight shifted against her, the leopard fell over backward with the man on top of her. This sudden movement released his arm and he instantly jammed his right fist, up to the elbow, down her throat. The cat began to strangle, and as she did so, Ake managed to work her front legs apart and get his knees firmly implanted against her ribs. With all his remaining strength, he rammed both knees into her rib cage until at last he heard a bone crack—then another, and another. The slobbering froth on her mouth began to turn a deep red, and Akeley knew that the broken ribs were piercing her lungs. Over and over again he brought his knees down hard on her chest with all the weight of his big body behind them, crushing her ribs one by one. At last her struggles slowed down until they ceased altogether and she lay still. Finally he slipped a hunting knife from his belt and plunged it into her heart.

Akeley made it back to camp. But as the expedition doctor was sloshing his mangled arm and shoulder with antiseptics, he keeled over in a dead faint.

"Boys," he said to his companions the next morning after he had come to, "that was an awful rough way to meet a leopard."

The newest star in the animal-training galaxy is a young man named Gunther Gebel-Williams, who is appearing, as this is written, with the Ringling show. Like Clyde Beatty, he is handsome and debonair—yet the only defense that he carries into the cage is a light whip and a soothing voice. In his act he combines lions, tigers, elephants, and horses—to create what the circus press agents describe as a "bizarre and breath-taking ballet."

Gebel-Williams was only twelve years old when he ran

away from home in Germany and joined a circus as a jack of all trades. But like all inborn animal men, he could not stay away from the big cats. One evening in Berlin, the regular animal trainer was ill and unable to go on. Gunther, who was just fifteen at the time, begged the ringmaster for an opportunity to do the act in his place. Such was his almost magical charisma with the beasts that he at once took complete charge. Since that first night, he has been a star with circuses all over the world. He is so devoted to his animals that he travels with them in the same railroad car between stands, and he feeds them, talks to them, soothes them, and pets them when they are caged in the back yard. For the finale of his act, he rides a giant Bengal tiger around the ring.

In the beginning years of the medieval European circus, the chief animal attractions were the trained bears. They walked upright on their hind legs, danced, and even managed to do simple rope-walking tricks. The big, clumsy bruins have never lost their crowd appeal. Nowadays they wear clown suits, ride bicycles or motorcycles, roller skate, and wrestle or box playfully with their trainers.

The black bears of both Europe and North America are easily tamed and trained if they are captured as cubs or are born in captivity. They are unusually intelligent, they learn their tricks quickly, and in spite of their great size and strength they often behave as docilely as dogs. Grizzlies, Kodiaks, and polar bears on the other hand are something else again. You will rarely see one of these species in a circus act. They seem to be totally without fear and cannot be intimidated by the crack of a trainer's whip or the blast of his blank-cartridge pistol.

One of the few acts involving these all but untamable beasts was presented by P. T. Barnum during the early years of his circus. James C. Adams, hunter and trapper

from the Rocky Mountain country, had managed to capture
and train about two dozen grizzlies—along with an assortment of black bears and wolves. Barnum billed the act
as "Grizzly Adams and His Trained Grizzlies," and exhibited it in a tent in a vacant lot on lower Broadway.

On opening day Adams paraded his animals boldly up
Broadway between cheering crowds. The parade was led by
a brass band. Dressed in the fringed buckskin clothes of a
frontiersman, he rode the largest and meanest of the bears
with a Western saddle.

Unlike later trainers, Adams beat his grizzlies into sub-
mission with heavy rawhide whips and wooden clubs. But
the bears were treacherous and unpredictable even after the
old man had punished them into going through their limited bag of tricks. Adams had been repeatedly mauled,
torn, and battered by the brutes—and one of them had
clawed away the top of his skull with one powerful swipe
of its great paw. On their first meeting, Barnum almost
fainted when the old mountaineer took off his coonskin
cap. Adams was slowly but surely dying from the effects of
the head wound when Barnum hired him, and he lived for
only another three or four months.

Next to the elephants and trained bears, the most charm-
ing animal acts in a circus—especially to small children—
are the almost-human chimpanzees. And the chimps are indeed nearly human in their behavior. Zoologists rate them
second only to man in intelligence.

According to naturalist Ivan Sanderson, chimps use their
brains just as humans do. And there are actual cases on
record in which chimps have worked out problems in reason-
ing better than men of average intelligence. One was a
famous experiment in which the problem was to get a
banana down from the roof of a room that was empty

except for a pole. The man poked at the banana with the pole until it fell to the floor and was smashed. The chimp set up the pole, climbed it, and got the banana down unbruised.

There seems to be almost nothing that chimps can't do except talk. They ride bicycles, motorcycles, and ponies; they juggle and perform incredible balancing feats. And, of course, they can skip lightly along tight wires as swiftly and surely as they run across the liana vines in their native African jungles.

Although horses are no longer the major circus attractions that they were in the days of Philip Astley and John Bill Ricketts, no circus is complete without them. Speaking generally, there are three kinds of horses that appear in circus rings.

First are the rosin-backs, so called by virtue of the fact that their backs are sprinkled with rosin dust to give the human performers a surer footing. These are the heavy, broad-beamed horses on which bareback riders and acrobat clowns do their equestrian acts. As a rule they are Percherons or Belgians, sturdily built draft horses whose ample backs offer a firm platform for the kinkers who are jumping on and off them, or turning somersaults and jumping through hoops as the horses lope slowly and easily around the center ring.

One of the most exciting rosin-back acts in the current Big One is a beautifully spotted Appaloosa stallion named Tiger who carries a big Bengal tiger on his back. Naturally he is heavily padded, for the tiger's claws would lacerate his back as the Bengal clutches for dear life to retain his balance. Tiger is visibly frightened half to death, and trembles all over when the tiger, whose name is King, leaps up upon him. But he goes through his act like a real trouper. It is with obvious relief that he trots out of the ring after the act is finished and the trainer has shooed the tiger back through the runway tunnel to its cage.

Liberty horses are shown in groups of from six to twelve or so, and perform their turns without riders. With gaudy harnesses and plumed headpieces, they go through their tricks at the command of a trainer who guides them by snapping a long whip over their heads or against their flanks. They trot proudly around the ring in circles, execute complicated reverse turns and letter "S" figures, stand up on their hind legs, dance in unison, and take graceful bows before making their exits.

The equine aristocrats of the circus ring are the *haute école*, or high school, horses. For the most part, these beautiful and talented horses are almost pure white. They are of a breed called Lipizzaner, a mixture of Arabian and European blood, which was developed at the world-renowned Spanish Riding School in Vienna. Whereas ordinary horses are full grown and able to be ridden at the age of two, a Lipizzaner stallion does not mature until he is at least four—and he reaches his peak when he is from ten to fourteen years old, an age at which most horses are well past their prime. Only stallions are used in *haute école* work. A pure-bred Lipizzaner stallion is born coal-black. Gradually his coat turns iron-gray and then pure white. It is not unusual for a Lipizzaner to live to be thirty or even forty years old, which is equal to about one hundred or more in the human life scale.

The Lipizzaner's style of performing is classic. He executes dance steps, side steps, high-stepping cakewalks, pirouettes and graceful bows. In horsemen's language, this kind of beautiful and difficult riding is known as *dressage*.

The side show has all but vanished from the circus scene, and the Wild West show has been pretty much replaced by rodeos and television horse op'rys. But as long as small boys spend long hours teaching their pet dogs to do tricks—as long as young people continue to be born who possess that elusive something known as a "way with animals"—the circus will always have its amazing and improbable animals and animal trainers.

Display #15

PINK LEMONADE—AND OTHER TALL TALES

"Pink lemonade!
Made in the shade!
For a pretty maid!"

For more than a generation in the old-time wagon shows, this was the favorite beverage which was sold to perspiring summertime circus-goers to wash down their peanuts and popcorn. But why *pink?*

Well—there was once an ex-clown named Pete Conklin who discovered that it was more profitable to make lemonade and sell it to the sweltering customers than to cavort around the ring in Joey make-up. No lemon ever found its vagrant way into his lemonade. He concocted it from tartaric acid, sugar, and a large chunk of ice to keep it cool.

One simmering afternoon in a small Southern town Pete found business so thriving that his supply ran out. He scurried into the back yard to get more water, but all he could find was a washtubful in which a lady acrobat had just rinsed out her pretty pink tights. He quickly mixed in his ingredients and set up for business again. The customers found the color of the lemonade so pleasingly different that thereafter Pete always added a harmless vegetable coloring to his product. Lemonade vendors in other shows followed suit—and "pink lemonade" became as much a part of the circus world as peanuts or elephants.

One day at the height of his nationwide popularity, the famous Dan Rice was riding a train across the prairies of Iowa when it was stopped and boarded by bandits. A pair of masked men entered the car and ordered all the passengers to hand over their money and valuables. One of them stared hard at Rice, then pulled down the bandana mask from his nose and grinned.

"Hello there, Uncle Dan!" he said. "It's nice to see you again." Then he thought for a moment. "Look here," he finally decided. "I used to sneak into your circus every time it came to Clay County, Missouri. So you just put that money and watch back in your pocket and we'll call it square."

"And what might your name be, young man?" the astonished Rice asked.

"Jesse James," replied the train robber.

When the Ringling circus was playing the Midwest around the turn of the century, the brothers were offered several thousand dollars by an organized group of crooks for the privilege of fleecing the show's customers by means of rigged gambling games and other assorted rackets. The Ringlings promptly kicked them off the lot.

At the next town on the circus schedule, the grifters retaliated by posting up on walls and telegraph poles what was without question the most unusual bill in all of circus history. It read:

When Thieves fall out, honest men get their dues!
    WARNING!
Neighbors, unchain your dogs!
Get out your shotguns!
Keep your children at home!
Lock all doors and windows!
    THE MARAUDERS ARE COMING!

They go by the name of Ringling Brothers!
They are Thieves, Liars and Scoundrels!
They have no show worthy of the name!
They plunder and steal!
We who give this warning are also thieves!
But we have fallen out with the greasy pack—
And now tell the TRUTH!

The grifters who paid good, if perhaps ill-gotten, money
to have the bills printed and posted at least told the truth
about themselves.

Charlie Ringling, next to the last survivor of the original
brothers, sometimes liked to drive in his automobile from
stand to stand instead of riding the circus train. One day,
whizzing across the California desert, he passed a broken-
down old Model-T Ford. An overalled farmer was gloom-
ily inspecting a flat tire as his wife and three or four small
children looked on. Charlie asked his chauffeur to stop and
see if they could help.

"All I need is some tire-patchin' material," the farmer
said. The chauffeur took some from his tool kit and helped
the farmer repair the damage.

"Where are you bound?" Charlie Ringling asked.

"Los Angeles," the farmer told him. "These kids have
never seen a circus and the Ringlings are playing there
tomorrow. It's the greatest show in the world, and I don't
want them to miss it."

Charlie took a notebook from his pocket, scribbled a few
words on it, tore out the page, and handed it to the man.

"When you get to the show grounds tomorrow," he said,
"give this to the man at the ticket wagon."

The farmer and his family arrived at the circus the next
afternoon to find the red-carpet treatment waiting for them.
Not only were they given the best front-row seats in the

tent free, but all the peanuts and popcorn they could eat and all the balloons the kids could carry away.

William Washington Cole, of the old Cole Brothers Circus, was a millionaire many times over. But even so he never let an opportunity slip by to pick up an extra quarter or half dollar.

One of his favorite gambits, just before the show began, was to spot a small group of people sitting in the "blues"— as the cheap general-admission seats at the ends of the big top were called—and join them. After a few minutes of staring around and stretching his neck, he would snort in disgust:

"Shucks! We ain't going to be able to see a dang thing from here. Let's all go and turn in our tickets for reserved seats. I don't care if they do cost more. I want a good look at the show."

Usually the people followed him to the ticket wagon, and after he had seen them pay extra money for better seats, he would go back to the "blues" to search out more people on which to try the same game.

Tom Kelly, a long-time veteran of the circus trail and now an executive with the Strates Shows, tells this one:

"Some years ago we had an alligator-skin young man in our side show. He sold pictures of himself to the customers. I told him he'd have to quit it because it was holding up the show, and I offered him an extra twenty-five dollars to make up for it. But he got mad, and talked one of my illusionists into double-crossing me.

"We had this illusion, see, what consisted of a midget hidden under a chair, lying down with his legs stuck out the front. Then we had a normal girl sitting in the chair so that it looked like she had two extra legs. We touted her as the four-legged girl. Well, one night after the alligator boy had got to her, the girl suddenly got up and walked off the stage, leaving the midget's legs dangling from the chair.

"The crowd began to yell, and I figured we'd have to refund their money. But then I got an idea. I had my wife walk out and sit in the chair to show the suckers how we worked this illusion. I said: 'This is our way of exposing fake freaks that are exhibited in other less ethical shows.'

"The crowd loved it. Everybody was happy with my explanation, and we didn't have to give back a single dime."

One time the Ringlings had an ancient lion that had lived long past his usefulness. While chewing on a bone one day he took too vigorous a bite, broke his jaw, and lost a couple of teeth. The circus veterinarian advised that the animal be destroyed for his own good. But Roland Butler, the current press agent, saw a heaven-sent opportunity for making headlines.

"We'll get the newspaper boys out here," he said in a moment of inspiration, "and you can operate on him in public."

The vet agreed, and the next morning a large group of reporters was on hand to witness the event. The vet, dressed in a doctor's white coat and wearing rubber gloves, entered the cage of the aged cat, gave him an over-sized dose of an anesthetic which knocked him out, and then proceeded to patch up the broken jawbone with wire and implant a pair of false fangs. The press was invited to return the following day to see how the operation had turned out.

The old lion never came out of the ether. He breathed his dying gasp during the night.

Next day the reporters were back on the scene. Butler was jubilant. He pointed to a healthy lion of middle age who was attacking a beef joint with gusto.

"Look there!" he said. "He's as good as he ever was. He's even better. He looks ten years younger. Yesterday you boys witnessed an entirely new breakthrough in medical science."

The story of the miraculous medical breakthrough was featured not only in all the local papers, but made the national wire services as well.

Press agents probably have more fun than anybody.

One morning Bill Doll "lost" twenty elephants in New York City's Central Park. For the first time in circus history, he had persuaded the mayor of the city to close the park to all vehicular traffic and allow bands, elephants, clowns, cowboys, tumblers, and other bespangled performers to parade from one end of the park to the other. But, very conveniently, he forgot to tell the bull-men when they should show up with their pachydermous pack. The elephants arrived an hour ahead of schedule. The thundering herd lumbered along, ambling happily through the trees and the byways—much to the delight of some thirty thousand children who had been given a school holiday to watch the procession—and it required several cordons of motorcycle and mounted policemen to round them all up and get them back to the starting point at 110th Street.

Thereafter the mayor of New York decreed that the parade through the park should be an annual event. But he made one strict stipulation. Doll would have to get the elephants at the park entrance at the same time that everybody else was there.

Another time, Doll arranged for a giraffe to be exhibited in the menagerie with its long neck bandaged from head to shoulder.

Newspaper reporters were curious. "What on earth happened to him?" they asked.

"The poor guy has a sore throat," Doll replied.

Next day, the sore-throated giraffe's picture appeared in every paper in town.

On one occasion, Doll invited the press to a champagne party on the evening before the show's opening. Several dozen writers showed up, eager to drink a few free glassfuls of the bubbly stuff. To the surprise and alarm of the Fourth Estate, the party was held in the lions' cage—with trainer Charley Baumann holding eight big snarling cats at bay with a whip and a blank-cartridge pistol. The gentlemen of the press gamely but gingerly entered the cage and sat down at the table. But nobody stayed for more than one fast drink.

Then there was the day Doll had his "second man," one Jake Meyer, plaster up posters on Grant's Tomb. Doll tipped off the police, and Jake was arrested. When they hauled him into court, the judge said sternly: "You know you can't put things like that up there!"

"Your Honor," Jake replied, "I knocked but nobody answered."

Tall stories sprouted up around P. T. Barnum as thickly as daisies flowering in a spring meadow.

One afternoon, a Mr. Louis Clark, who was an editor with a sophisticated New York magazine called the *Knickerbocker,* dropped into the Barnum museum.

"Friend Barnum," he asked, "is it true that you have in your collection the actual war club that killed Captain Cook?"

(Captain James Cook, by way of explanation, was the famed English sea dog and explorer who discovered the Hawiian Islands and was killed there by hostile natives.)

Barnum rose to the bait like a hungry trout rising to snap at a May fly.

"Why, yes," he said. "It so happens that I have that very club. If you will wait here for a minute, I will get it for you."

He leaped up the stairs to a collection of South Seas war clubs that was there and selected the biggest and most brutal-looking one that he could find—a club that looked as if it could indeed have killed Captain Cook, or for that matter anyone else who might have happened to get his head into the path of its swing. He hastily attached a label to it that read: "The Capt. Cook Club," and carried it down to Clark.

"Poor Captain Cook," Clark sighed, hefting the heavy weapon in his hands. "Are you sure this is the authentic club?"

"Indeed it is," Barnum replied proudly. "I have documents to prove its identity beyond all question."

"Well, Mr. Barnum," Clark said seriously," I am much obliged to you for letting me see this fearful weapon. I have been in half a dozen other smaller museums in this and other cities, *and since all of them have it,* I was sure that such an excellent establishment as Barnum's museum would not possibly be without it."

When Tom Thumb was the star of the Barnum show, it was playing one day in Washington during the time of the Civil War. Abraham Lincoln invited the mighty midget to the White House for lunch.

"General," the President asked, using Tom's circus title out of courtesy and perhaps amusement, "how do you think the war is going?"

"Mr. President," Tom replied without batting an eye, "my friend Barnum could get the whole thing settled in a week."

Phineas Taylor Barnum exerted an almost mystical impact upon the circus-going people of his day and age.

The old showman liked to go on the road with his circus whenever he could—and he preferred to sit in the midst of the audience where he could hear the comments of the country people.

On one balmy afternoon in Erie, Pennsylvania, he was seated in the "blues" directly behind a farmer and his wife.

"Mercy sakes, Sally, I do declare," he overheard the man say, "I never did think it possible to see such wonderful goings-on as we've seen here today."

"There's one thing I'd like to see more than the whole show," the woman replied, "and that is Barnum himself. I hear that he travels sometimes with his circus."

"Well, maybe we *will* see him."

In a few moments a young equestrian dashed into the ring, riding four bareback horses at once. Horses and rider went through their routine to perfection, and to thunders of applause. For a grand finale, the youthful rider turned a somersault, landed with his head and arms on one of the horses' backs, and rode triumphantly around the ring with his heels in the air.

The old farmer jumped to his feet, swung his hat over his head, and shouted: "I'll bet five dollars that's Barnum his own self. There ain't another man in America who could do a thing like that but Barnum!"

In telling the story later, Barnum wryly remarked: "I did not disabuse his mind. I felt that he had gotten his money's worth, and we both were satisfied."

The circus itself is a fantasy land—and it breeds its own tall tales.

Display #16

THE SHOW THAT NEVER GROWS UP

For all its twentieth-century trappings, the circus today is like the boy who never grew up. The show you go to see this summer hasn't changed much in its essentials from the one that Grandpa and Grandma stared at goggle-eyed when they were kids.

There is a good deal more of everything. The acts are more complicated, the equipment more modern, the costumes more glittering. The big top is likely to be a huge indoor arena rather than a tent. But the elephants still waddle ponderously around the ring carrying pretty girls in their trunks. They still balance on tiny tubs and clumsily stand on their heads. The horses dance and prance. The acrobats still fly on the swinging trapeze and walk precariously along the high wire. The Joeys look just like they always have, as they clown their way through the old tried and true routines. The bands still blare out ear-shattering music. The lions and tigers still roar and snarl and are as scary as ever. The butchers (circus lingo for peddlers) still go up and down the rows of seats hawking their peanuts, popcorn, pop, and souvenirs. There is the same sense of wonderment, the same circus smell, the same glistering, mysterious mixture of sawdust and star dust in the air as there has always been.

Except for a few of the biggest ones, most of the nearly one hundred circuses that still show across the country today have forsaken the rails and gone back to traveling the roads—just as Aaron Turner and Barnum and the Flatfoots did. The only difference is that instead of slogging through the mud and dust of unpaved and unmarked rural byways, they now speed along modern superhighways in caravans of trailer-trucks.

In our modern America, Ringling Brothers and Barnum & Bailey stands astride the circus world like a colossus. With its dual units, its thousands of performers, its carloads of animals both wild and tamed, the Big One truly deserves the title that was born more than a century ago in the fertile brain of P. T. Barnum—the Greatest Show on Earth.

Foreign shows, notably the Moscow Circus, which is perhaps the biggest and most sensational circus in Europe, come to the States every year or so and play in auditoriums in the major cities.

But the day of the small-town circus is far from gone. Nearly every community of any size at all still gets to enjoy its once-a-year Circus Day. Some two dozen of these smaller shows still play under canvas. The others exhibit in ball parks or indoors.

Selling methods had been streamlined. Nowadays, most circuses are sponsored by civic organizations such as the Shriners or the local Rotary or Lions' Club. The club guarantees the circus a minimum box-office take, out of which it shares the profits for charitable purposes. Anything over the minimum goes to the circus management. A few are underwritten by commercial companies, and the admission charge is one or more labels from the company's product plus, as a rule, half the price of a regular ticket. These latter are known to circus people as "box top" shows.

Just as there has always been, there is still a lot of fierce competition between circuses for routes, dates, and show places—and some of it is still pretty ruthless and cut-throat. But it is a more refined and gentlemanly ruth-lessness and cut-throatedness. The old "rat bill" type of dog eat dog—on which Barnum, Forepaugh, and Sells Floto flourished—is a thing of the past.

Aside from Barnum and Bailey and the Ringlings, a few of the old-time circus names have survived to our modern day—for example the Clyde Beatty-Cole Brothers Circus, the Sells and Gray Circus, and the King Brothers Circus. The idea of the word "brothers" in a circus title has persisted from the long-ago times of the Flatfoots. In addition to the Coles and the Kings, there are the James Brothers (no relation to Jesse and Frank), the Polack Brothers, the DeWayne Brothers, the Graham Brothers, the Kay Brothers, the Miller Brothers, the Rudy Brothers, the Royson Brothers, and the Hoxie Brothers (who boast the only Negro animal trainer in the current circus world).

Among the better-known little-big (or big-little) circuses on the road today are the Hubert Castle Shows, the Tom Packs Circus, the Famous Bartok Circus, Gatti-Charles, Carson & Barnes—the only circus left that puts on a daily street parade because it plays only in very small towns—and the James Hetzer European Circus—which is European largely by virtue of the fact that it shows under canvas and in only a single European-style ring instead of the traditional American three rings. The James A. Strates Shows are a gigantic combination of carnival and circus which employs nearly as many people as the Big One —and travels from stand to stand in a fifty-car railroad train.

These are only a few of the shows that merrily carry on the tradition of the old sawdust trail. But they are glittering, glistering proof that the circus will be with us always.

The circus is a fabulous wonderland of make-believe that no one—old or young—can resist. For a brief afternoon or evening, it takes you into another world.

The band strikes up its overture.

The house lights dim. Blaring spotlights dot the arena with sprinkles of diamond dust.

The clowns begin their walk-around.

You can see the horses and the elephants and the bespangled kinkers waiting for the Grand Entry.

The ringmaster, clad in a brilliant blue cape, steps up to the microphone, doffs his top hat, and sings out:

> *"La-dees and gentle-men!*
> *"Children of all ages!*
> *"It's circus day today!*
> *"Welcome one and all!*
> *"Welcome to—*
> *"The Greatest Show on Earth!"*

And for all us unreconstructed circus buffs, that is just precisely what it is.

INDEX